Eric Gill.

£5=

PR

ENGLISH SPAS

1 Bath: Sydney Gardens in 1805
From the aquatint after J. C. Nattes

ENGLISH SPAS

By
William Addison

B. T. BATSFORD LTD.
LONDON   NEW YORK   TORONTO   SYDNEY

By the same Author :

Essex Heyday

The English Country Parson

Epping Forest—Its Literary and
    Historical Associations

The Worthy Doctor Fuller

First Published *1951*

Printed and bound in Great Britain by William Clowes and Sons, Ltd.,
London and Beccles, for the Publishers
B. T. BATSFORD LTD., LONDON: 15 North Audley Street, W.1 & Malvern Wells
Worcestershire; NEW YORK: 122 East 55th Street;
TORONTO: 103 St. Clair Avenue West; SYDNEY: 156 Castlereagh Street

PREFACE

DR. WILLIAM FALCONER of Bath, who wrote in the eighteenth century, said that in his day there were already more than a thousand treatises on mineral waters. One might almost suspect that these precious streams ran ink instead of water. And the ink as well as the water continues to flow, until by now the accumulated books and pamphlets would as effectively defy analysis as the waters themselves, apparently, invite it. It is therefore surprising that while so much has been written on the medical side of spa life, little has been written on the social side. It is true that Bath has a large and comprehensive literature. But the social history of the spas collectively is scattered through a multiplicity of books—novels, memoirs, letters, journals, reminiscences, guide-books, as well as through a variety of unpublished sources. To trace all such references would be a laborious task, and the present work aims at being pleasurable rather than laborious. For all that, it is hoped that the search has been sufficiently diligent to produce a balanced and detailed picture of a phase of English life which, though fresh as ever in the pages of Jane Austen, Smollett, and Ned Ward, is already fading from the public mind. The origin of most of the spas in pre-Reformation holy wells—a somewhat neglected subject—has been dealt with, and their place in modern society has been considered; but the main purpose of the book has been to study and re-create the life of their most brilliant period, which began with the Restoration and ended with the Regency.

W. A.

LIST OF ILLUSTRATIONS

LIST OF ILLUSTRATIONS

ACKNOWLEDGEMENT

The Author and Publishers wish to express their thanks for permission to reproduce the following illustrations:

The Birmingham Public Library (Sir Benjamin Stone Collection), for Figs. 67 and 68; the Trustees of the British Museum, for Figs. 11, 27, 45, 46, 48, and 62; Messrs. The Campden Gallery Ltd., for Figs. 31, 47, 51, 52, 60, and 61; the National Portrait Gallery, for Figs. 28, 64, and 65; Mr. Edward H. Pinto, for Fig. 14; the Royal Mineral Water Hospital, Bath, for Fig. 63; Messrs. Walter T. Spencer, for Figs. 4, 9, 21, 33, 53, 54, 55, and 56; the Victoria and Albert Museum, for Fig. 36, and (from the Enthoven Collection) for Figs. 18, 19, and 20.

CONTENTS

2 From a Colour print of 1817

3 From an engraving after J. Hassell, 1795

BATH PANORAMAS

4 'A Modern Belle going to the Rooms at Bath'

From a print of 1796

Chapter One
TAKING THE WATERS

Some drink of it, and in an houre,
Their Stomach, Guts, and Kidneys scower:
Others doe Bathe, and ulcers cure,
Dry Itch, and Leprosie impure;
And what in Lords you call the Gout,
In poor the Pox, this drives all out.

From a poem in *Musarum Deliciae* (1655) entitled
'To a Friend upon a journey to Epsam Well.'

IT is true, as Matthew Bramble in *Humphry Clinker* remarked to Dr.
Lewis, that 'There are mysteries in physic, as well as in religion;
which we of the profane have no right to investigate.' It is also true
that in the history of the spas, which Matthew Bramble had in mind, the
two mysteries are related in that when the saints went out the doctors came
in. The spas began as holy wells—pools and springs where men prayed
first and were healed afterwards. How they were healed was a mystery; but
the cure, it was thought, came from the saint, not the water. At the
Reformation, when the saints were no longer allowed to have mysteries,
the holy wells became wishing wells. The profane as well as the devout
love mysteries, but less ardently. Consequently there were fewer cures, and
by Cromwell's time, when most of the wells were neglected, the saints
were despised and the cures forgotten.

Water is not in itself an exciting topic. Hippocrates might be thought to
have said all that need be said about it when he remarked that those waters
are most proper for use which are clear, light, and void of taste and smell.
But the most popular spa waters had none of these negative qualities. They
were heavy and coloured; they stank; they were distinctly a cultivated taste.
Yet because they were thought to cure gout, dropsy, and all the effects of
late nights and large dinners—as well as making childless women able to
become mothers—they were drunk with enthusiasm long before science had
discovered how to use them medicinally. It was not until 1825—that is to
say, not until the spas were declining as centres of fashion—that a reliable
method of analysing their waters was established. Nor was the body itself

correctly analysed in the seventeenth century. It was still thought of in terms of the four fluids: blood, phlegm, choler, and melancholy. These were the four humours; but they were anything but mirth-provoking. Choler was known as yellow bile, melancholy as black bile, and Tunbridge boasted that its waters were a sovereign remedy for the latter. One of its favourite seventeenth-century doctors, Dr. Madan, was most eloquent on the subject. The Tunbridge waters, he said, 'with their saponary and detersive quality, clean the whole microcosm or body of man from all feculency and impurities. No remedy is more effectual in hypochondriacal and hysterick fits by suppressing the anathymiasis of ill vapours, and hindering damps to exhale to the head and heart.' The mediaeval had not yet been exorcised from the scientific mind. Such verses as those of John Lydgate in the fifteenth-century *Falls of Princes* would have gone perfectly well into a seventeenth-century work, and they, indeed, may have come from the fourteenth-century Boccaccio:

> *These bathes to soften sinews haue*
> *Great vertue and to scoure the skin;*
> *From morphew white, and blacke to saue,*
> *The bodies faint, are bathde therein.*
>
> *From leprye, scabs, and sores are olde,*
> *For scurfes, and botche, and humors fal,*
> *The bathes haue vertues many folde,*
> *If God giue grace to cure them all.*

Boccaccio, with his amorous tales, his flair for the comical and the extravagant, is a fitting shade to invoke in such a subject as this; but first the collective name of these watering places ought to be explained. It comes, we are told, from a Walloon word, *espa*, a fountain, and is taken from Spa, the Belgian town sixteen miles south-west of Liége, known to veterans of the First World War for its occupation by the Germans on the 4th August 1914, and as the Kaiser's headquarters four years later. As an indication of the great antiquity of Continental spas, as compared with English, it is worth noting that the Belgian resort was founded in 1326 by Collin le Loup, an ironmaster of Liége who was cured by its chalybeate springs. Many other springs on the Continent were famous between two and three hundred years before the English began looking for them at home. The Romans, we know, used Bath and Buxton. But organised spas on the Continental model came with the Cavaliers and survived to the Regency. About 1830 they lost their first fine careless rapture and became respectable. Indeed, in the nineteenth century, with their terraces, parades, and gardens, they became the acme of respectability. They were hardly that earlier. In the Regency they were the places where the sexes, with undisguised ebullience, displayed themselves to each other most seductively. Seen from the nineteenth-century view-point we may say that they flourished in a naughty age. But seen from an earlier view-point—an Elizabethan, shall we say—the gallantries at Bath and Tunbridge Wells would seem almost boring. What counts is that if we follow the line of their development from Elizabethan to Victorian times we see how important they were in the evolution of polite society. The roistering Elizabethans would hardly have been abashed by the good manners of Caroline revellers; but they would have had difficulty in returning the compliments of the dandy and the beau. When Beau Nash was the arbiter of taste, the Tudor wench already belonged to a barbarous and half-forgotten age. She would have shocked the world of 1750 as much as the unblushing baggage of 1750 was to shock the demure and simpering miss of 1850. None of them, of course—except, perhaps, the simpering miss—would have shocked the girls of 1950.

It would be unwise, however, to take conduct at the spas as representative of English society as a whole at any particular time. The Abbé Le Blanc, in *Lettres d'un Français* (1745), discusses the transformation effected in English ladies by the waters of Bath—or some other local agency still more potent. They became, he says, new creatures, casting off 'the constraint and melancholy imposed upon them by the yoke of habit during the rest of the year in the Capital,' and for one glorious and by no means virtuous month enjoyed a nature-cure that was as primitive in fact as in appearance—by artfully calculated deception—it was made to look civilised. Le Blanc, apparently believing that the English Camilla was at heart no different from the French coquette, explained her abandonment of reserve by observing: 'The fair patient has had to feign illness, to win over the servants, to corrupt the doctor, to persuade an aunt, to deceive a husband, in a word to resort to all sorts of artifices to succeed. She naturally seeks compensation for all the trouble she has taken.'

But although both their collective name and their original character came from the Continent, for reasons that will be explained presently, the development of spa life in England was characteristically English. With our chronic perversity, having become far more solemn than our neighbours in health we became far more jovial in sickness. The Abbé Le Blanc noticed this. He said: 'They are much deceived who think that the waters of Bath are like those of Bourbon, where only infirm, paralytic or valetudinarian persons are to be found. This is the place in all England to enjoy good health, and to turn it to account.' Eleven years earlier the Abbé Prevost had noticed the same thing. If the people he met had illnesses, he remarked, they were evidently not of a kind to interfere with enjoyment.

The first amusements introduced at the spas were probably innocent enough. They were devised to relieve the tedium of a life of leisure to people who were not used to it. That later these amusements became far from innocent merely proves again that 'Idleness is the devil's bolster.' The sixteenth-century Harrison of Radwinter has nothing whatever to say about this high life at the spas in his *Description of England*. On the contrary, he derives patriotic satisfaction from the contrast in behaviour between the bathers at our English establishments and those at their Continental equivalents, 'whereof,' he says, 'some write more a great deale than modestie should reveale and honestie performe.' He wrote before 1577, when there was little or no Continental influence at the English wells, though in the *Faerie Queen*, written only ten years or so later, we have a reference to 'th' English Bath, and eke the German Spau.'

This question of the early amusements at the spas is discussed in a book, *Englishmen at Rest and Play*, written by Members of Wadham College,[1] in which we are reminded that as early as 1572 Dr. Jones, in *The Benefit of the Auncient Bathes of Buckstones, which cureth most greevous Sicknesses, never before published*, describes galleries for walking in, and for use in playing an indoor game called 'Troule in Madame,' apparently a cross between bowls and bagatelle. For outdoor entertainment Dr. Jones recommends bowls and archery. Even music, which was to become so notable a feature of spa life, already had its place in the new way of life, for Dr. Jones says delightfully: 'Before you enter the Bath, tary two or three dayes, as well for resting of you, after your long travayle, as also to acquaint you with the ayer, using some melody, the which thing *Aesculapius* worthily appointeth, saith *Galen*, and indeed it refresheth the witte, encreaseth strength, and melancholy it putteth to flight.' Similarly Dr. Deane of York (1626), writing of Knaresborough and the Harrogate neighbourhood, says, 'After dinner they ought to use no violent exercise, neither ought they to sit still, sadly, heavy, and musing, nor to slumber, and sleepe; but rather to stirre a little, and to raise up the spirits for an houre or two, by some fit recreation. After supper they may take a walke into the fields, or Castle yard.'

It was not until the Restoration that the spas slipped out of the control of these sober and well-meaning doctors. The Cavaliers had livelier ideas. Charles II and his cronies discovered that at Epsom, Bath, and Tunbridge

[1] Oxford University Press, 1931.

Wells they could escape from the oppressive responsibilities of London, and live again the carefree life they had known on the Continent. Whatever may be the most important discovery in the medical history of the spas, this is the most important discovery in their social history. The king and his court were not the only persons seeking relief from the excessive sobriety of Cromwell's New Order. Nor were the idle rich the only ones who followed suit. The populace were as eager as their prince for merriment. And it was not the waters they wanted. They resorted to the spas as they had formerly resorted to country fairs. The spas catered for them in the same spirit. Dealers in knick-knacks, toys, and trinkets were to be found in all of them. In the spas near London the poor were able to buy odds and ends for a few coppers, while in such places as Bath and Tunbridge Wells, catering as they did for wealthier patrons, jewellery and expensive curios were bought and sold freely. It was a romantic age and fairings were in demand. Love-making, both real and affected, was the order of the day. John Macky, in *A Journey through England in Familiar Letters from a Gentleman Here to His Friend Abroad* (1714), tells us that on Box Hill it was 'very easy for Gentlemen and Ladies insensibly to lose their company in these pretty labyrinths of Box-wood, and divert themselves unperceived . . . and it may justly be called the Palace of Venus.' The amorous propensities of the Cavaliers had early directed the pursuit of pleasure at the spas in a romantic direction.

As we should expect in so indulgent a world, the pleasures of the table were not wanting. At Tunbridge, according to the same Mr. Macky, a particular delicacy was the Sussex wheatear, which he describes as 'the English ortolan, which is a very dear bit at the Wells, but is the most delicious morsel for a creature which is but one mouthful, that can be imagined.' He was not the only writer to comment on the gastronomic delights of Tunbridge. Congreve, in a letter to Dennis the bookseller, dated 11th August 1695, wrote: 'You would not think how people eat here; everybody has the appetite of an ostrich, and as they drink steel in the morning so I believe at noon they could digest iron.'

But in spite of all these counter attractions the waters were drunk, and with a will. There was a sort of ritual about the process. The Dr. Madan already quoted said: 'In reference to the number of glasses, you may make it either odd or even; though some who are of opinion that all things are composed of number, prefer the odd before the even; and attribute to it a greater efficacy and perfection especially in matters of physic. Wherefore it is that many doctors prescribe always an odd pill, an odd draught or drop to be taken by their patients. As seven planets, seven wonders of the world, nine muses, God is three and one.' To-day such discussions sound more like the language of the medicine man, or tribal magician, than that of the medical practitioner.

One of the most renowned of the early doctors recommending water cures was Dr. Lodwick Rowzee, who practised at Ashford in Kent and wrote a book entitled *The Queenes Welles* (1632). In this curious work he gives directions to those who wish to drink to the best advantage. 'Now concerning the time of the day,' he says, 'the morning, when the Sunne is an houre more or lesse high, is the fittest time to drinke the water. For when the Sunne beginneth to be of force, it doth attract some of the mineral spirits, and the water loses some of its strength.' Like other early writers on the subject, he also recommended exercise. 'Those that lye not too very far from the Springs, and are able to use their legges,' he says, 'shall doe better to come thither afoote, than to ride, because so they shall heate their bodies more. Yet doe I not intend they should be so hot, as to sweate, or to be readie to sweate, for that would doe hurt, but I meane onely that their naturall heate should be something awaked or excited, because then the water will be the better attracted, and have the more speedie passage.' After drinking the waters, the patient was again expected to take a turn on the Pantiles: 'It will doe well to walke and stirre there up and doune,' the doctor continues, 'and to compose your selfe to mirth with the rest of the companie; For those that looke to reape benefit by *Tunbridge*, must turne away all cares and melancholy.'

But it is in the quantity he recommends that Dr. Rowzee takes our breath away. 'Now for the whole quantity of water to be taken in a morning, you shall see some that rise very high, even to three hundred ounces,[1] according to Nestor's years; yea, and some a greater quantity. And it is a thing that will make the very women there filling their glasses to laugh, to see some patients sent thither by ignorant physicians, and appointed to take ten or twelve ounces of water, and arise perhaps to twenty or thirty ounces.[2] But this may be a rule for a body of competent years and strength, to begin at thirty, forty, or fifty ounces, and to arise by degrees, increasing their quantity every day, to a hundred, an hundred and fifty, or two hundred ounces,[3] more or less, as they shall be able; and so again to decline and decrease by degrees, ending where they began.'

In course of time this excessive drinking ceased, and in 1738, a hundred years after the publication of Dr. Rowzee's book, we find Francis Hare,

[1] Eighteen pints three gills.
[2] About one pint three quarters.
[3] From six pints and a half to twelve pints and a quarter.

Bishop of Chichester, writing to his son: 'They used formerly indeed to drink two quarts at Tunbridge and Bath, which would make eighteen good glasses, but not large ones. But our physicians now unreservedly condemn that practice, and do not prescribe above a pint.'[1] These later physicians probably discovered that a pint was as much as their patients would endure. When we read of quantities rising to twenty pints at a sitting being ordered by some of the early doctors at Tunbridge Wells, we can only feel relieved that a dash of healthy cynicism towards the medical profession crept in. Otherwise the patients would have become as water-logged as a Cambridge fen.

As soon as the novelty had worn off, water drinking lost its appeal, and the average patient treated his doctor's prescription with the amused, if respectful, scepticism that the Englishman normally has for professional men. The properly constituted Englishman never forgets that doctors are human, and practise in private, even if they do not preach in public, that soundest of all the maxims of health—'A little of what you fancy does you good.' They must have smiled to hear Dr. Rowzee, himself an inveterate smoker, not only allowing but commending tobacco, even with the absurd proviso that the smoke should be held in the mouth for a few minutes before being puffed out. A building known as the Pipe Office was erected near the spring at Tunbridge, in which, for a subscription of half a crown a season, a pipe could be hired for use daily. This later became the Gentlemen's Coffee House. Again with Dr. Rowzee's approval, breakfast rooms were provided for use after early morning dips. The genial doctor, in giving his blessing to the enterprise, confessed: 'I never was able to fast with patience until noon, but must needs cast a bit to my barking stomach before the rest of my company went to dinner.' So quite early it was decided that the waters were for the patients and not the patients for the waters.

Once that principle was settled, there was no limit to the recreational possibilities of the spas, or to the company they might attract. In *Tunbridge Walks, or, The Yeoman of Kent*, played at Drury Lane in January 1703, the question is asked: 'What company does the place afford?' and Reynard, a gentleman who lives by his wits, replies:

'Like most publick Assemblies, a Medley of all sorts, Fops Majestic and Diminutive, from the long flaxen Wig with a splendid equipage, to the Merchant's spruce 'Prentice that's always mighty neat about the Legs; 'Squires come to court some fine Town-Lady, and Town-Sparks to pick up a Russet-Gown; for the Women here are wild Country-Ladies, with ruddy Cheeks like a Sevil-Orange, who gape, stare, scamper, and are

[1] *Hist. MSS. Com. T. J. Hare's MSS*, 241.

brought hither to be disciplin'd; Fat City-Ladies with tawdry Atlasses, in defiance of the Act of Parliament; and slender Court-Ladies, with French Aprons, French Night-Cloaths, and French Complexions.'

This account of the mixed company to be found at the spas is worth noting, because it draws attention to the country women as well as to the court ladies. It tells us that the two were now mingling in a new way. Hitherto, town life for the landed families had been lived in London or one of the provincial capitals, country life in country houses. The old market towns belonged to rural, not urban, life. Up to now the two orders of society had been separate; but when the Court went down to Epsom and Tunbridge, London moved into the country and urban life was superimposed upon rural life. It may be remembered that Eustace Budgell, Joseph Addison's cousin, wrote to the *Spectator* because he was so uneasy about the propriety of introducing country dances into polite society. It seemed inelegant to allow the rough and tumble of the village dance to displace the stately minuets and gavottes, then so precise and disciplined, though these also had once been country dances. But after the middle of the eighteenth century it was obvious that, for a few seasons anyhow, the spontaneity and gaiety of the country dance would be more attractive to the young than the more refined steps could be. Indeed, within a few years the country, that seemed so barbarous to a previous generation, had been romanticised beyond recognition, and people, apparently intelligent, professed to believe with Cowper—in spite of all the devilry recorded in parish documents—that 'God made the country and man made the town.'

But Eustace Budgell died when Cowper was only six, so he was too early in date to be converted to belief in the New Innocence. Some of the dances he complains about sound delightful. There was 'Hunt the Squirrel,' in which the girl ran away from the man, then suddenly turned on her pursuer and he was obliged to flee from her. Mr. Budgell saw nothing reprehensible about this, though he was surprised to see his daughter display more boldness and familiarity with the young men present than he had thought her capable of. But shortly afterwards the fiddlers began to play for 'Mol Patley,' a dance in which the young man whisked his partner off the ground so indelicately that Mr. Budgell, who sat upon one of the lowest benches, 'saw further above her Shoe' than he thought proper. 'Therefore,' he says, 'just as my girl was going to be made a Whirligig, I ran in, seized on the Child, and carried her home.'

When such dances as 'Hunt the Squirrel' and 'Mol Patley' were introduced in the spas, we can imagine how popular they would be with the

5 'This is what we call the cold pillip, Sir!'

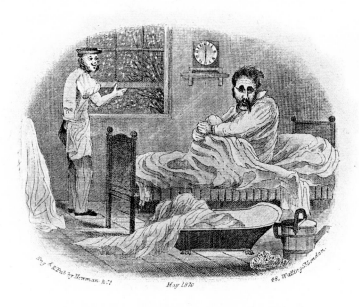

6 'Now Sir, jump up—It's six o'clock—The sitz bath
and the wet sheet are quite ready, and the doctor says
you are to have the window open!'

A VICTORIAN WATER CURE

7 'This is the way we are treated, as if we were garden shrubs'

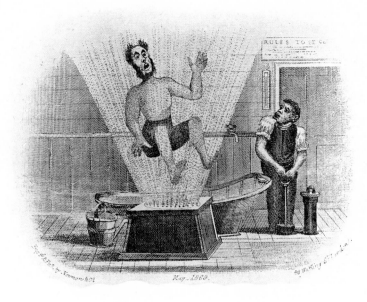

8 'The ascending douche—"Now Sir, do sit still"'

A VICTORIAN WATER CURE

blasé young bucks of the day for their novelty and vivacity. But we can also imagine how disturbing they were to parents, and how offensive to men of taste. 'These watering-places,' said Horace Walpole, 'that mimic a capital, and add vulgarisms and familiarities of their own, seem to me like Abigails in cast gowns, and I am not young enough to take up with either.'[1] He evidently failed to notice that they did in fact give an advantage to age:

> With patches, paint, and jewels on,
> Sure Phillis is not twenty-one!
> But if at night you Phillis see,
> The dame at least is forty-three.

Perhaps Horace Walpole was afraid of being attracted by such a Phillis of apparently twenty-one who turned out to be forty-three! But seriously, in these urban pleasures the brain counted for quite as much as the body: a new assessment of parts in English society, where field sports—weight throwing, and similar lusty games—had previously been thought the only amusements beseeming a man. At the spas, to the advantage of the ageing, physical prowess, instead of being watched with applause, was thought clumsy and uncouth. Effeminacy and foppishness crept in, as we shall see later, and the last state was worse than the first; but it was all to the good that at last the brain did count.

Eventually, indeed, wit became master, as it had never before been master in England; and nowhere else did it enjoy such licence. The young, of course, then as always, paid court to beauty; but the ageing had at last won a place for themselves, where they could enjoy each other's brilliance, knowledge of the world, and social influence. There were, no doubt, many old roués who took unfair advantage of their newly won liberties. 'Lord Berkshire,' the charming blue-stocking Elizabeth Montagu tells us, writing in 1740, 'was wheeled into the room on Thursday night, where he saluted me with much snuff and civility, in consequence of which I sneezed and curtseyed abundantly; as a further demonstration of his loving kindness, he made me play at commerce with him. You may easily guess at the charms of a place where the height of happiness is a pair royal at commerce and a peer of fourscore.'

In this new sort of life that was not quite town and not quite country, some kind of compromise had to be agreed upon. In dress, for example, the leaders of fashion had to decide whether to adopt a casual or a formal costume. Eventually, the casual won, but for a long time the two alternated. The problem of social barriers appears to have been solved early, perhaps

[1] Horace Walpole to G. Montagu, 6th October 1766.

because it hardly existed for the Cavaliers. It was agreed—as Smollett shows in *Ferdinand Count Fathom* and Scott in *St. Ronan's Well*—that however intimate two persons might be at the wells, they should completely forget each other on returning to town. So far as memory went, the waters they drank were the waters of Lethe:

'But you knew me at the Wells, my lord,' said a man of low degree on meeting a pump-room acquaintance in St. James's Park.

'Then, sir,' retorted the peer, 'I shall know you again—at the Wells.'

Into this new and uncharted reach of society came every kind of rogue and pretender. Previously, London had been the only place in England where a livelihood could be won by gaming. Goldsmith, in his life of Beau Nash, describes the scene. He says of London: 'To this great mart of every folly, sharpers from every country daily arrived for the winter, but were obliged to leave the kingdom at the approach of every summer in order to open a new campaign at Aix, Spa, or the Hague. Bath, Tunbridge, Scarborough, and other places of the same kind here, were then frequented only by such as really went for relief; the pleasures they afforded were merely rural, the company splenetic, rustic, and vulgar. In this situation of things people of fashion had no agreeable summer retreat from the town, and usually spent that season amidst a solitude of country squires, parsons' wives and visiting tenants, or farmers; they wanted some place where they might have each other's company and win each other's money, as they had done during the winter in town.'

The company at the spas was not as rustic as Goldsmith suggests at the time he had in mind; but certainly as they developed the spas did provide a new field for gamesters, and it was one of these, Beau Nash himself, who finally determined their character. By the sheer force of his personality, he gained an ascendancy over the society of Bath and Tunbridge Wells that enabled him to impose his will upon every phase of their life. Under his rule, Bath got a code as strict as our own highway code, and no judge could have more authority in a twentieth-century law court than this Master of Ceremonies had in eighteenth-century Bath. Yet he was a man of little education and of insignificant birth. We shall see how he did it when we talk about Bath. But on the fact of his authority, here is Goldsmith's evidence: 'I have known him on a ball night strip even the Duchess of Q—— and throw her apron at one of the hinder benches, observing that none but Abigails appeared in white aprons. This from another would be an insult, in him it was considered as a just reprimand, and the good-natured duchess acquiesced in his censure and with just good sense and good humour begged his "Majesty's" pardon.'

Of this novel and amusing life, with a gamester as king, we have innumerable descriptions. It was wholly conventional and never quite sincere. Much of its piquancy was in its many teasing subterfuges. It was a game rather than a life, and its rules had to be followed from getting up in the morning to going to bed—not always the right bed—at night. Mrs. Elizabeth Montagu said that so far as she could see it consisted of 'How d'ye does?' all morning and 'What's trumps?' all night. But there was more in it than that. Here the waters were used externally. So first came the baths, in which the men usually wore drawers and jackets; the women, linen costumes, with their heads in chip hats. They were carried to the baths as a rule in sedan chairs, and on arrival each lady furnished herself with a small wooden receptacle, in which she could put her handkerchief, and perhaps her snuff box and patches. This she took into the water with her. Mrs. Montagu describes the scene thus: 'Handsome, japanned bowls floated before the ladies, laden with confectionery, or with oils, essences, and perfumery for their use. Now and then one of these bowls would float away from its owner, and her swain would float after it, bring it again before her, and, if he were in the humour, would turn on his back and affect to sink to the bottom, out of mere rapture at the opportunity of serving her.'

After strolling about in the warm and steaming water for an hour or so, the bathers were carried back to their rooms, where they dressed and at once returned to the pump-room in a casual sort of costume called *deshabillé*. Here Mrs. Montagu's 'How d'ye does?' were exchanged over hot drinks until breakfast, which might be either public or private. Normally it was private; but a distinguished personage staying in the town would often invite guests to breakfast with him in the assembly-rooms. When the coffee houses were established it became the custom for gentlemen to adjourn to these and read their newspapers. The morning's high spot was a service in church, which was something of a farce:

> Now for pure worship is the church design'd,
> O that the Muse could say to that confin'd!
> Ev'n there by meaning looks and cringing bows,
> The female Idol her Adorer knows.
> Fly hence, Prophane, nor taint this sacred place,
> Mock not thy God to flatter Celia's face.[1]

The pretence, in Bath at all events, may not have lasted long, for in the *Gentleman's Magazine* for 1760 we find: 'Not long since at Bath the Subscription Books were opened for Prayers at the Abbey and gaming at the

[1] *A Description of Bath* (1734), p. 10.

Rooms. In the evening of the first Day, the Numbers stood as under, and occasioned the following Thought:

> The Church and Rooms the other day
> Open'd their books for pray'r and play;
> The priests got twelve—Hoyle sixty-seven,
> How great the odds for Hell 'gainst Heaven.

After service there was shopping, changing of library books, a stroll on the heath, a drive for the elderly, and for the young a canter on the downs, moor, or whatever the common adjoining the spa was called. This was the most free and recreational part of the day. After dinner, which might be any time between two and three-thirty, everyone was expected to dress for formal strolling along the parades and exchanging of compliments until tea was ready in the assembly-rooms. For the evening's entertainment there would be gambling, dancing, or the theatre. It was the same routine at all the fashionable spas—Bath, Buxton, Harrogate, Scarborough, or Tunbridge Wells, and later at Malvern, Cheltenham, Leamington, and the younger spas.

The company, too, was the same in all. And all had much in common topographically. Where possible, an amphitheatre of hills was expected in the background, romantically broken by rocks that were a trifle too stagey in effect, shaded by trees, equally theatrical, which afforded the 'pleasant shade' and 'pleasing prospects' so dear to the eighteenth-century heart. The hills, incidentally, must have been cruel to patients crippled with rheumatism. Horace Walpole, who was not a lover of spa life, complained of these hills that 'run against one's nose,' so that one 'cannot stir out without clambering.'

The development of the spas scenically was curiously parallel with their development socially. Tunbridge Wells, as an early example, had the mixture of rusticity and formality already observed in its social life. Even as late as 1779 we find Samuel Cripps writing from the Wells to Fanny Burney ('dear Fannikin') that the houses 'are scattered about it in a strange, wild manner, as if they had been dropped by accident, for they form neither streets nor squares.' It seems odd to us in the twentieth century that the very towns that we now regard as our most successful experiments in town planning should once have been criticised for being formless, yet it did take a time for people to get used to the idea of having open spaces and avenues of trees in the centre of a town. Later, though the terraces, crescents, and parades, rising tier by tier from pump-room, assembly-room, and gardens became formal enough, any natural feature, such as a river, was always brought into the scheme, and the inspired development of these became the major attraction of the spas when they had matured into fashionable inland resorts, which, though by that time their waters appealed only to a minority of their visitors, were still called watering-places.

After Drinking the Water

Chapter Two

EPSOM AND
TUNBRIDGE WELLS

The rendezvous of ffooles, Buffoones & Praters,
Cuckolds, Whores, Cittizens, their Wives and Daughters.
OLD RHYME

I

THE first flush of English spa life at its most riotous and bibulous
befell Epsom and Tunbridge Wells. Epsom was infected first; but
the two had a deal in common. 'It is now a Rumbling Time of the
year, and the gentlemen being most of them gone out of town, Tunbridge
and Epsom and such Places were full of People,' says Defoe in *Moll
Flanders*. The special virtues of the Epsom waters—in the medicinal, not
the moral sense—are said to have been discovered towards the end of
Elizabeth's reign, when a pond on a common west of the village was used
to cure ulcers. No one drank the Epsom waters—that is to say, the medicinal
Epsom waters—before about 1620. Fuller, in the Surrey section of the
Worthies, relates how the famous Epsom spring was discovered in the dry
summer of 1618 by a farmer named Henry Wicker (or Wickes), who
noticed that a hole made by an animal's hoof filled with water. By poking
with his stick he saw that there was a small well; but what astonished him
was that the cows, thirsty as they were, refused to drink, though the water
was perfectly clear. This seemed odd, so he had a sample analysed, and was
told that it was impregnated with a bitter, purging salt, which the learned
then called calcareous nitre, now call sulphate of magnesia, while the rest
of us call it Epsom Salts. Of the subsequent renown gained by these
purging waters, Fuller says with his usual shrewdness: 'Their convenient
distance from London addeth to the reputation of these waters; and no
wonder if citizens coming thither, from the worst of smokes into the best
of airs, find in themselves a perfective alteration.'

This well that brought London to Epsom, and made it the first of our

English week-end resorts, is still to be seen in the garden of a house called 'The Wells' in Woodlands Road, on the edge of Epsom Common.

Aubrey, who drank these Epsom waters in 1654, puts the date of the discovery as late as 1639-40. In doing so he may have been thinking of their discovery by the people of London, for the third Lord North, who discovered the Tunbridge spring, claimed in his *Forest of Varieties* (1645) to have popularised Epsom as well. Certainly the two developed together, for we find that a course at Epsom was frequently recommended as a preparation for a course at Tunbridge. The one, being nearer London, could be taken as an experiment, before the patient, if he benefited, moved to the other for longer treatment. Its accessibility also made Epsom preferable for men of affairs who had to keep in touch with the City. Thus it became the businessman's special resort. The *London Gazette* of the 19th June 1684 announced that the post would go daily betwixt London and Epsom for the convenience of those who were drinking the waters. Pepys, as we should expect, knew all about them. In the Domestic State Papers for 29th June 1668 we find a letter addressed from Chatham Dockyard by John Owen to Pepys, begging leave of absence for twelve days in order to take a course of Epsom waters. In the following August he begged further leave. Samuel himself was at Epsom—though not to stay—in the July of both 1663 and 1667.

On his 1663 visit Pepys found 'a great store of citizens, which was the greatest part of the company, though there were some others of better quality.' That so many of these citizens, as he called them, could afford Epsom was an eye-opener to him. 'But, Lord!' he says, 'to see how many I met there of citizens, that I could not have thought to have seen there: that they had ever had it in their heads or purses to go down thither.' In the account of his 1667 visit we have that joyful passage that every husband chuckles over, in which he confides that he and his wife were up at four in the morning in order to make an early start; but Mrs. Pepys, to her impatient Samuel's annoyance, spent so much time dressing that it was 'past five o'clock before she was ready.' For all that, they did get off, amply provided for the journey with 'bottles of wine, and beer, and some cold fowle,' in a coach-and-four that carried them safely to the wells by eight. Pepys, anxious as ever to put his time to the greatest profit, drank four pints of the water, filled bottles to carry home with him, gossiped with the women at the well, who told him that they rented it of the lord of the manor for £12 a year, and generally picked up all the news he could. He put up at the 'King's Head,' which still stands on the south side of High Street, where he chatted about Parson Fuller—the worthy Doctor himself—and where, no doubt, he picked up that nice bit of gossip: 'hear that my Lord Buckhurst and Nelly are lodged at the next house, and Sir Charles Sedley with them: and keep a merry house. Poor girl! I pity her.'

In this last remark he strikes the note for the gay and licentious Epsom that came into being about this time. The house referred to is now the 'Nell Gwyn Café,' and while she stayed there Nell is said to have used a secret door, still shown, between the house and the inn. The association of this vivacious lady with Epsom was no less happily continued when she exchanged her Charles I, as she called Lord Buckhurst, for Charles II, for it was the latter who built her the stables in Church Street, now a private house called The Farm.

The rapid development of Epsom in Charles II's reign came with the demolition of Nonsuch Palace, given by Charles in 1670 to Barbara Villiers, who was created Duchess of Cleveland that year, and quickly converted by that unscrupulous lady into cash. In other words, the palace became a quarry, from which stone was sold to build smaller houses. Some of the ornaments of the palace are still to be seen in the town. The two stone lions, for example, surmounting the columns at the entrance to Pit House in Church Street, which dates from this period, are said to be such. Epsom thus became one of the first residential towns in England, developed for the benefit of the rich merchants of the new commercial age, who by this time had become sufficiently prosperous to be able to afford two houses, one in the city and one in the country. The lord of the manor seems to have regarded these changes with favour, for about 1690 he began to lay out the town with avenues of trees, and, with an eye to the revenue that might accrue from the spa, built a ballroom seventy feet long. Houses were built specially for visiting invalids. Inns multiplied. Waterloo House, at the west end of the south side of High Street, formerly the 'New Inn,' was built in Charles II's reign to receive the more fashionable of the new visitors, and part of it served as the spa's assembly-rooms. Later, it is sad to relate, the principal room degenerated from being the scene of quadrille and minuet to providing a ring for Sunday afternoon cock-fights. The 'Spread Eagle' was one of the several seventeenth-century inns at Epsom that were enlarged in the eighteenth century to serve the spa; but it was never as large as the 'New Inn,' which is said to have been at one time the largest tavern in England.

Celia Fiennes describes for us the town as it was at the beginning of the eighteenth century. She says that the place was 'cluttered with company' from Saturday to Tuesday, but was quiet enough during the rest of the

9 TUNBRIDGE WELLS in 1748. Among the figures represented are Dr. Johnson, Colley Cibber, Garrick, Beau Nash, and other celebrities of the time

From an engraving of 1804 after the contemporary painting by Thomas Loggon

10 The Park in Regency Times
From an engraving after George Shepherd, c. 1825

11 The Pantiles in the Eighteenth Century
From the painting by Thomas Loggon

TUNBRIDGE WELLS

week. The spa did not attract her. The well was unpaved and, being covered with a wooden building, so dark that she could not see whether the water was clean or not. She alleged that when the supply gave out, water was carried to it from common wells with no medicinal virtue. Indeed she thought the well-house more like a dungeon than anything else. But she found several good houses in the town and approved of the gardens.

The daily routine would be that already described, with one or two particular local attractions, such as racing on the downs, in a ring similar to the one in Hyde Park. This was at noon, and was followed by foot-races, wrestling matches, and other country sports. One of the most popular of these was trying to catch a pig by the tail, and according to the *Tatler* of the 30th June 1709 such an announcement as that 'several Damsels, swift of foot, will run a race for a Sute of Head Clothes at the Old Wells' would be sure to draw all the sparks of the neighbouthood to the scene of the contest. On a fine Sunday evening there would be as many as seventy coaches in the ring—the present race-course—while any evening a motley company could be found card-playing, gambling, and misbehaving generally. In Shadwell's comedy, *Epsom Wells,* which began a long run at the Duke's Theatre in 1673,[1] the society of Epsom is described as being composed of 'impertinent ill-bred City-wives' staying at the well with 'their tame Husbands, who gallop hither upon their Tits, to see their faithful Wives play a game of Ninepins, and be drunk with stum'd wine; and strait are gone to their several and respective vocations.' So loose did life become here that Shadwell's Lucia could say 'The freedom of Epsom allows almost nothing to be Scandalous.' One of the most amusing scenes in the play shows Mr. Woodly pursuing two masked women—masks being then the fashion—and on catching them being discomfited to find that one was a sixty-year old woman 'with a wrinkled, pimpled face, but one eye, and no teeth,' while the other was his own wife.

Epsom's curtain rose on a scene well set and gaily lighted. But there was one part badly cast, and that the main one. Its doctor, Levingstone by name, planned and built a new Epsom, sinking in 1704 a second well, which he surrounded with ball-rooms, raffling-rooms, 'attended every day by a fine consort of musick,' and, of course, a pump-room. Shops were provided for jewellers, milliners, toymen, a bookseller, and all the essential trades, and these displayed their wares so attractively that for a time the Epsom shops were said to rival those of London. One or two of these shops remain to-day, with gracious bow windows to remind us of these palmy days of the eighteenth-century spa. Dr. Levingstone also provided a bowling green, arranged

---

[1] *Tatler,* No. 7, April 1709.

cock-fights and horse-races, and did everything, it seemed, to make the New Wells a profitable concern for himself, and a pleasurable one for everyone else. Hackney carriages and sedan chairs were seen everywhere. As a final measure to secure, as he thought, the success of his scheme, he bought the lease of the old wells, and closed them. Then, as a last noble gesture, he announced that the water in the new wells he had provided so generously would be supplied free of charge. Alas! he had no thanks. The water was worthless.

After this fiasco, the fortunes of Epsom depended on elements other than water. The god of chance became the tutelary genius of the town. The well failed; but the race-course succeeded. And after the founding of the Derby and the Oaks at one of the Earl of Derby's house parties towards the end of the eighteenth century Epsom's renown was in something more durable, if no less fickle, than water. The town has a curious history, but the queerest thing about it is that here where virtue was all too rare, the water was so pure that nobody wanted it.

A rollicking description of Epsom in 1711, by John Toland, author of a sceptical treatise entitled *Christianity not Mysterious,* though rather disconnected, conjures up the scene as it was when Prince George of Denmark, consort of Queen Anne, was a frequent visitor. It is quoted by Aubrey in his *Natural History of Surrey.* Epsom, we learn, was then a bright little town, 'everywhere mighty neat,' with modern houses built behind long avenues of limes and elms, the branches of which were intertwined to form porticos and arbours where breakfast could be served, or supper, and where a cheerful glass could be enjoyed over a pipe in the afternoon. Celia Fiennes describes this fashion of cutting trees. She says: 'there are great curiosities in cut hedges and trees almost before all doors; they have trees in rows which they cut up smooth, and about three or four yards up they lay frames of wood in manner of a penthouse, so plait the branches on it and cut it smooth; they leave the stem of the tree to run up and then cut it clear to the top which they cut in round heads.' There is still an archway of clipped yews over the garden gate of 'Yew Tree Cottage' in the High Street to remind us of this local custom.

From Toland we learn that there was a paved terrace at Epsom—similar, no doubt, to the Pantiles at Tunbridge Wells—where the coffee houses stood. The drinking of coffee, introduced into England in 1667, was then the height of fashion. 'By the conversation of those who walk there,' says Toland, 'you would fancy yourself to be this minute on the Exchange and the next minute at St. James's; one while in an East India factory, or a West India plantation, and another while with the army in Flanders, or on

12 Epsom: from the Race Card for 1st June 1827

board the fleet in the ocean. Nor is there any profession, trade, or calling that you can miss here, either for your instruction or for your diversion.' Here, he goes on, the beauties of the day shine like stars, 'not half so much by their precious jewels and costly apparel as by the more pointed glories of their eyes. Here every old man wishes himself young again, and the heart of every youth is captivated at once, and divided between a thousand deserving charms.... In the raffling-shops are lost more hearts than guineas.... There you'll see a sparkish young fellow of twenty-five, sitting right over a blooming beauty of eighteen; but so intent on gain and the dice that he never exchanges a word or a look with her; while a little lower you may smile at an old hunks, that loves his money as well as any in the city, yet loses it as fast as he plays, by having his eyes wholly off his cards, and fixed on a green girl of thirteen, that cares as little for any man there as he does for his wife at home.'

Echoes of Toland are to be found everywhere in the literature of the spas. Who can doubt that Macaulay had that worthy's book before him when he wrote those sparkling paragraphs on Tunbridge Wells in the third chapter of the *History of England*? It is from Toland that we get those refreshing pictures of the country folk bringing their produce to market: 'the choicest fruits, herbs, roots and flowers, with all sorts of tame and wild fowl, with the rarest fish and venison, and with every kind of butcher's meat, among which Banstead Down mutton is the most relishing dainty.' He delights us with an account of the 'fresh and artless damsels' from the surrounding villages, 'striking their bargains with the nice court and city ladies, who, like queens in a tragedy, display all their finery on benches before their doors.' Some of the ladies even had the market girls up to their bedrooms, where they brought the day's supplies for the kitchen, and then, after a dish of chocolate perhaps, settled down for another nap.

Epsom may well be proud of its literature. It has a good passage in Macky's *Journey through England*, and Defoe writes of its downs: 'covered with coaches and ladies, an innumerable company of horsemen, as well gentlemen as citizens...the racers flying over the course, as if they either touched not, or felt not, the ground they ran upon; I think no sight, except that of a victorious army, under the command of a Protestant King of Great Britain, could exceed it.'

For a time all went well with Epsom in spite of Dr. Levingstone; but like so many other resorts it had its on and off seasons, and in the *Ambulator* of 1782 we read: 'The hall, galleries, and other public apartments, are now run to decay; and there remains only one house on the spot [the old well] which is inhabited by a countryman and his wife, who carry the waters in bottles to the adjacent places.' Hunter, in his *History of London and Environs* (1810) says of Epsom that 'except during the time of the races few places can be more dull and uninteresting.' No doubt this would depend upon the point of view. The residents may have preferred the quieter part of the year. Nevertheless they could hardly fail to feel a measure of pride in being associated with races as famous as the Derby and the Oaks. There is no need to describe what these races meant to the nineteenth century while we have Frith's 'Derby Day' in the National Gallery as a visual record. But the downs have other delights, as anyone may see for himself who visits them at week-ends, and on them, of course, stands Epsom College, founded in 1855 by John Propert.

Though it has lost its place as a spa, Epsom, in addition to its place as a racing centre, still retains the character as a residential town that it gained so early. What other towns and villages were to become after the rapid expansion of London following the Industrial Revolution, Epsom already was, with the difference that it was able to bear itself in the new world with a dignity it had acquired in the old—a dignity so many of its rivals lacked. So with a house such as Durdans, home of the Earls of Rosebery, and several fine old inns, Epsom has had more to teach the twentieth century than to learn from it. Durdans stands between Woodcote Road and Chalk Lane, and the family's association with Epsom is preserved in many ways, notably in Rosebery Park, the gift of the Earl in 1913. The town has its faults, of course. As John Toland put it, 'Even Venus had a mole; and gossiping is the greatest objection I have ever heard made to Epsom.'

II

It has already been made clear, that to provide a genial environment for the enjoyment of bad health has always been a primary purpose of the English spas. Tunbridge Wells, high on the Kentish Weald, 420 feet above sea level, with its huge blocks of freestone rock tumbled on a sandy common, was one of the first to be discovered, and at once set the style in successfully combining solicitude for health with the pursuit of pleasure. Its discoverer, Dudley, third Lord North, set a worthy example by preserving his own enfeebled condition for more than sixty years. He lived to be eighty-five.

The story begins in 1606, with Lord North riding through the forest where Tunbridge Wells stands now, from Lord Abergavenny's shooting-box at Eridge, two miles away. He was then in his twenty-fourth year, but his constitution had been undermined by a futile attempt to keep pace with the swaggering hard-drinking Scots, who had standards of revelry beyond the compass of softly nurtured Englishmen. His doctor prescribed country air, and where could he have found better?

From this forest dwelling, Lord North rode out one morning like a mediaeval knight, attended by his servants, through what Aaron Hill describes as 'an assemblage of all Nature's beauties,' and came to a spring whose waters left a gleaming deposit on the ground they washed. Had he, in fact, been a mediaeval knight instead of a dissipated young peer, he might have mistaken the deposit for gold. As it was, he was reminded of the water at Spa, the Belgian watering-place he had passed through while serving with volunteers in the Low Countries a few years earlier, and sent one of his servants to borrow a drinking bowl from the only cottage near. A few sips and he was satisfied that the two waters had much in common. Bottles were brought and samples of the water sent to London, where the experts reported that after dropping into it as much powder of galls as would cover a two-penny bit, the water blushed, which apparently denoted not modesty, but the presence of 'vitriol.' It could therefore—according to the science of the day—be recommended as a cure for colic, melancholy, and the vapours. The most curious thing about it was that besides killing flat worms in the belly, loosening the clammy humours of the body, and drying the brain, it would make both the lean fat and the fat lean.

All this was much to the satisfaction of the Lords North and Abergavenny, who cleared the woods round the springs, sank wells over the two largest, paved them, and enclosed them with rails. Lord North, however, was thoroughly English in his valetudinarianism, for in 1638 he wrote: 'There is more danger of the physician than of the disease.' His lordship was no fool. 'Do we not daily see the poorer people fall sick and recover; whilst the richer make themselves a sacrifice to the physicians' art and tyranny?' he wrote.

The fame of the new wells quickly spread among the country people; but Tunbridge Wells was not established as a spa until the visit of Queen Henrietta in 1630. There were then no suitable houses to accommodate her in, so timber cottages and huts had to be brought in on sledges, and tents set up on Bishop's Down Common, part of which was cleared for them. She came to recuperate after the birth of Charles II, and stayed six weeks, passing the time with masques, dances, and such entertainment as she had been accustomed to enjoy at Continental spas, most of which were innovations in England. Booths were erected near the wells, and each day, as at Epsom, the buxom country girls came in from the Kentish farms with their cream, cherries, wheatears, and quails, to behold the wonder of so many maids of honour and gallant young courtiers enjoying this long midsummer picnic. The common is still romantic enough for us to imagine the scene as it was in 1630, when the queen and her court transformed this Kentish woodland into a Forest af Arden.

But, after all, this mediaeval chivalry and midsummer madness could only be a passing phase, and Tunbridge Wells as we see it now was established on much more durable foundations. As with all these spas, a patron —if not always a patron saint—came forward in the guise of a medical man. Dr. Rowzee, whose book on the proper conduct of water-drinkers has already been mentioned, praised the waters eloquently, and Dr. Madan supported him by arguing the necessity of drinking them on the spot. 'Waters once removed,' he alleged, 'lose their vivisick spirits in which a virtue doth reside, which afterwards no diligence can restore. Chalybeate waters in long deportation will not tinge with gall.'

The terraces later to be known as the Pantiles were levelled in 1638 as a promenade for the water drinkers. Along them was planted an avenue of elms to afford shade to the market people who stood there displaying their produce (11). Shopping was always the morning occupation of the ladies, most of whom bought their own supplies. The lower walk was full of booths, where butchers, poulterers, fishmongers catered for the tables of visitors. Each morning they were joined by the fresh-complexioned country girls in their clean linen aprons and chip hats, who stood beside their baskets of farm produce. Along the upper walk milliners, jewellers, haberdashers, booksellers, most of them from London and there for the season only, provided for more aesthetic needs. At first both shops and stalls were of slight construction, and in 1687 most of them were destroyed by a disastrous fire which may have burnt the trees along one side. They appear to have gone about this time. Perhaps they had become a nuisance, and were cut down when brick shops were built here after the fire.

How these terraces came to be called the Pantiles we shall see in a moment. Meanwhile we may well be puzzled by other names in the town. What connection can there be between gout and Sion, for example? or Mount Ephraim, another local name? The answer is that both these names date from the time when the Roundheads and the Royalists had camps in Tunbridge, the former at Rusthall, the latter at Southborough. The spas were then regarded, and not without reason, as possible rallying points for Royalist sentiment. So for several years Cromwell's Ironsides kept watch on the hills they named Sion and Mount Ephraim.

Any hope of turning this Cavalier playground into a Puritan bethel vanished with the Restoration. In 1663 Queen Catherine of Braganza, in the pathetic hope that the waters would enable her to bear a child, visited both Tunbridge and Bath. Chalybeate waters had the reputation of promoting fertility, and the alarming result of the visit was that though the queen herself was proof against them, her ladies, apparently, were not.

Queen Catherine was far better housed than Queen Henrietta had been. She lodged on Mount Ephraim in a house lent by Sir Edmund King, his Majesty's physician. Others of her retinue were accommodated in houses in the neighbourhood, while the rest encamped in tents on the common. Each morning they went down to the wells, and after taking the waters chattered and laughed together under the spreading branches of the elm trees while they bought gloves and stockings at the shops, or tried their luck at the raffling booths, for the habit of raffling had been brought over from Paris and was already established at the Wells. Gambling and flirting were the order of the day, while each evening the entire company would assemble at the bowling green for open-air dancing on the smooth, dry turf. On special evenings a company of players would be summoned by the Queen, partly for love of the play, and partly in the hope that her ladies in gossiping with the actresses would pick up news of how Miss Stewart or Nell Gwyn stood with the king at present. But there was danger with these actresses. Even under the Queen's eye Prince Rupert was paying court to Margaret Hughes, and losing all interest in graver matters. In 1678 a comedy, *Tunbridge Wells*, written by 'A Person of Quality,' was produced, and the *Dramatis Personae* is a sufficient indication of the kind of society by that time to be expected at the Wells. There is Tom Fairlove, 'a gentleman of the town, that loves handsome women'; Owmuch, 'a gamester that lives by his wits and borrowed money'; Mr. Wilding, a stylish husband who indulges in a few indiscretions; Sir Lofty Vainman, who is all that his name suggests; Squire Fop; Parson Quibble; Poet Witless; a pampered alderman's wife; and two whores, Brag and Crack. The play, whether justly or not, shows what Tunbridge Wells represented to the popular mind at that time:

> The ladies make choice by the size,
> The gallants by Garb and Proportion,
> And when the brisk Spirits do rise,
> They fall to their carnal devotion.

Church-going became the fashion at this time, and the church of St. Charles the Martyr, with its heavily moulded ceiling, remains to remind us of the days when the House of God was little more than a salon.

> You all go to Church upon hearing the Bell,
> Whether out of Devotion yourselves can best tell.[1]

[1] *Tunbridgiale*, p. 8.

13 Tunbridge Wells: The Parade, about 1825

From a contemporary print

14 Tunbridge Wells: The Pantiles, in Tunbridge Ware

The Pantiles recall Queen Anne, the third royal lady to be associated with the Wells. Whatever the cause of her visit, it cannot have been the same as Catherine's. She brought seventeen children into the world. But all were weakly, and only one survived infancy. This was William, Duke of Gloucester (1689-1700), and it was probably for his sake that the 1697 visit was paid. At that time the promenade was unpaved and when the duke fell and hurt himself on the stones, the princess—as she was then—handed a hundred pounds to a cottager with instructions to level and pave the walks before her next visit. She picked her man badly. When she came again nothing had been done, and she was so annoyed that this was her last visit, though Tunbridge not only tiled the walks (and thirteen of the original pantiles can be seen in front of the well to this day) but also planted a triple row of birch trees on Bishop's Down Common to celebrate her coronation, calling it the Queen's Grove.

Strolling along the shady Pantiles (9), with its flower-baskets, its tile-hung and weather-boarded shops and restaurants, it is still easy to recapture the spirit of eighteenth-century spa life. Reclining in a deck-chair one can imagine the time when, as Rochester has it:

> Here Lords, Knights, Squires, Ladies and Countesses,
> Chandlers, and barren women, Sempstresses,
> Were mixed together; nor did they agree
> More in their Humours than their Quality.
> Here, waiting for Gallant, young Damsel stood,
> Leaning on Cane, and muffled up in Hood:
> The would-be Wit, whose business was to woo,
> With Hat removed, and solemn scrape of Shoe,
> Advances bowing, then genteelly shrugs,
> And ruffled Foretop into Order tugs.

Perhaps the recreation of past glories will be accomplished more easily with closed eyes. The old musicians' gallery—still there—may then be imagined without the modern band-stand near it. The assembly-rooms and the pump-room can be seen as they were when they served their original, not their present, purposes. Instead of twentieth-century tourists we may see Dr. Johnson, Beau Nash, Lord Chesterfield, Pitt, Garrick, Richardson, Goldsmith, and the future Duchess of Kingston step across the walk as they do in the print of 1748 (9). And here in one small particular I must beg to differ from Miss Barton, to whose delightful and admirable history of Tunbridge Wells[1] all who follow her must be indebted, in

[1] Margaret Barton, *Tunbridge Wells*, Faber 1937.

hesitating to claim the first figure in the print as the only Dr. Johnson worth having in such company. That he had not at that date been made a doctor means nothing. It was almost as common then to give a man of such learning a courtesy doctorate as it is now to give one to a medical practitioner, M.D. or not.

By the middle of the eighteenth century, life at Tunbridge Wells had settled into a rigid order. By then the place had become what to some extent it remained, waters or no waters, the resort of the serious-minded. No other English town of its size has produced such a stream of dilettante literature. Describing these writers in the *Guardian* in 1713, Richard Steele wrote: 'The Water Poets are an innocent tribe and deserve all the encouragement I can give them. It would be barbarous to treat those writers with bitterness who never write out of season and whose works are *useful* with the waters.'

Everyone, apparently, wrote verses at Tunbridge. Its society was the most literary in England outside London, and if most of these poetical effusions were of little value as poetry, some were admirable as records of contemporary life. One of the best descriptions we have of spa life is a rhymed epistle from a clergyman at Tunbridge Wells to a lady of his acquaintance in London. It tells us, for example, how the tradesmen came out from the Wells to Tonbridge and Sevenoaks, touting for orders:[1]

> *No muse's aid I durst convene,*
> *To paint the clam'rous babel scene;*
> *For sure no muse was ever there,*
> *Where twenty tongues at once declare*
> *Their diff'rent trades, and diff'rent names,*
> *While each your sole attention claims.*

The butcher presents his compliments and confides that:

> *He serves my Lord and Lady P.,*
> *Will hit your palate to a T.,*
> *And, by the chaplain's benison,*
> *For mutton gives you venison.*

The pastrycook, who serves the Prince of Wales, and has the plumes over his door, is even cockier than the butcher.

Nothing escapes this reverend chronicler's eye. Nor does he hesitate to describe the gaming-hall, where the gamesters

> *display their skill*
> *At cribbage, whist, or dear quadrille,*

[1] The word *touting* is said to come from Tooting, the village to which the traders and race-course touts rode out from Epsom.

26

and, having completed his tour of the village, he leads his lady out in imagination to 'rude romantic rocks'...

> *Where sylvan Dryads haunt the grove,*
> *And playful Naiads wanton rove.*

The ceremonial aspect of life at the spas always appealed to the clergy, though it was not one of their number who ordained it. The strict, though far from virtuous code of behaviour at Tunbridge Wells was introduced by Beau Nash, who came from Bath when over sixty, bringing the formidable Sarah Porter with him. For the remaining twenty years of his life he remained its Master of Ceremonies.

As the presiding muse, however little of the Parnassian there was about her, Mrs. Porter, the 'Queen of Touters,' succeeded the illustrious Mrs. Causey, who died in 1735. There were many other local 'characters' during the eighteenth century, notably Beau Fielding, of whom Theophilus Lucas wrote in his *Memoirs of the Gamesters* (1714): 'He was generally trick'd up in Gauderies, as if he had resolved to make the whole Female Sex his conquest; and by his varieties of Fashions his very Creditors durst never swear him to be the Man they had trusted. Every step he took presented you with a perfect Puppet Play; and Rome itself could not in an Age have shew'd you more Antics than this notorious Fop was able to imitate in half an Hour.' There were also visitors and residents who were as ridiculous in their gravity as the dandies were in their gallantry. Mr. Reginald Lennard in *Englishmen at Rest and Play* (pp. 58-9) quotes from a manuscript in the British Museum:

> *For here it was my cursed luck to find*
> *As great a ffop tho of another kind:*
> *A tall stiffe fool that walkt in Spanish Guise,*
> *But lookd as grave as Owle, as Woodcock wise:*
> *The buckrom puppet never mov'd its eyes.*
> *He scornes the empty talking of this mad age*
> *And speakes all Proverbs, Sentences & adage*
> *Can with as much solemnity buye eggs*
> *As a Caball doth talk of their Intreagues,*
> *Master of Ceremony yet can dispence*
> *With the formality of talking sence.*
> *From hence strait to the upper end I ran*
> *Where a newe Scene of ffopery began:*
> *A tribe of Curatts, Priests, Canonicall Elves*
> *(Fitt Company for none besides themselves)*

Were gott together, each his distemper told—
Scurvy, Stone, Strangury, some were so bold
To charge the Spleen to be their misery,
And on that wise Disease brought infamy.

These drinkers of the graver sort were not always left to the company of their own kind. There were times when they might be seen arm in arm with the dandies. Any morning about the middle of the eighteenth century Colley Cibber, a jaunty foppish figure, could be met on the Pantiles in company with the doleful Dr. Young, author of *Night Thoughts*. Later in the century the gay tended to give place to the grave, and Tunbridge Wells developed as a highly respectable residential town. By the end of the century it had gained such favour with the well-to-do that it was well embarked on the career that was eventually to make it one of the wealthiest, if not, indeed, *the* wealthiest residential town in the country. The change from one kind of life to another did not come suddenly; but as Brighton waxed, Tunbridge waned. For a generation or more the leisured and rich moved easily between coast and country, with no particular preferences for either. Both had the same amenities. Mr. Baker, the Tunbridge Wells bookseller, opened a shop at Brighton, and the doctors, not to be outdone by a bookseller, followed suit, even to the extent of declaring that the waters of both towns had the same properties. Both Brighton and Tunbridge Wells had shops full of knick-knacks, leaving, however, Tunbridge its fame for odds and ends in tesselated woods, a most interesting local craft (14). But gradually the young came to favour the newer resort, and Tunbridge was left largely to the elderly and those who preferred the country, for, after all, the woodlands, furzy commons, and surrounding villages of the Kentish weald were assets not easily matched.

Then, early in the nineteenth century, the town took a new stamp with the development by Decimus Burton of the Calverley Estate on Mount Pleasant to a design well suited to the needs of the new age. This transformation may be said to have been completed when in 1835 the old spa village became a town. Henrietta the vivacious, and Catherine the saturnine, with their gay young ladies, light of heart and light of love, were forgotten. The walk once paved with Queen Anne's pantiles was now paved with stone flags and called 'The Parade.' Donkey-riding was the fashion, in which, instead of Brighton taking its cue from Tunbridge, Tunbridge took a hint from Brighton. The town was no longer rakish. But it was still in keeping with the tastes of the nation's ruling house, and the local Museum has that delightful picture of Queen Victoria as an infant princess, taking a donkey ride on the common in 1822, her head protected by a parasol. She returned often, and always loved the place, a favour that Tunbridge Wells acknowledged by continuing to represent in society the virtues that will always be associated with her long and prosperous reign.

A Cardiac Complication —

15 *From a drawing by Randolph Caldecott*

Chapter Three

COCKNEY ARCADIA

Now sweethearts with their sweethearts go
To Islington, or London Spaw;
Some go but just to drink the water,
Some for the ale which they like better.

POOR ROBIN'S ALMANACK

I

THE cockney, quick as ever to adapt himself to the manners of a new age, soon had spas at home. Two of them, Sadler's Wells (17) and Islington Spa (18), aped their betters and called themselves The New Tunbridge Wells, a name that was still to be read under the coping of No. 6, Lloyd's Row, until this and neighbouring houses were reduced to rubble by enemy action during the Second World War. The site is now occupied by the block of flats facing both the theatre and the offices of the Metropolitan Water Board. The two spas were within a stone's throw of each other; but were separate establishments. Their use of the same name, however, and that not an honest one, has led many writers on London to confuse them, even since their distinction was pointed out in the *Gentleman's Magazine*, in 1813. Islington Spa was much the more important of the two. In grounds extending from the present Spa Green,

Time was when satin waistcoats and scratch wigs,
Enough distinguished all the City prigs,
Whilst every sunshine Sunday saw them run
To club their sixpences at Islington.[1]

According to M. Misson, a Frenchman who published an account of his travels in England at the end of the seventeenth century, the waters could 'do you neither good nor harm,' provided you drank them in moderation. The gardens, which opened about 1680, were spacious and inviting, with rows of lime trees and the usual arbours and shady retreats. Evelyn, who visited them in 1686, must have approved of what he saw, though appar-

[1] Charles Jennings.

ently he did not trouble to say so. But the arboreal delights that Evelyn would note were not to be Islington's major attraction. The people came neither to drink the waters nor to walk in the gardens, though some did both. The majority came chiefly to throw the dice, which here was thought 'a gentlemanly game.' Warwick Wroth describes the scene in *The London Pleasure Gardens*. 'Sir Courtly Nice,' he says, 'drove up to the gate in his gilt coach, and old Sir Fumble brought his lady and daughter. Modish sparks and fashionable ladies, good wives and their children, mingled with low women and sempstresses in tawdry finery; with lawyers' clerks, and pert shopmen; with sharpers, bullies and decoys.' There was dancing to the strains of a string orchestra every morning from eleven to twelve, and Mondays and Fridays in the afternoon. The swell of the spa was a conceited beau called The Tunbridge Knight, one Martin by name, who strolled round the gardens with a yellow cockade on his hat, carrying on his fist a hawk named Royal Jack.

While elegant in a rakish kind of way, Islington was a veritable Paradise for every kind of mountebank. Quacks abounded—among them the Dr. Misaubin with his famous pills mentioned by Fielding in *Tom Jones*.

According to her own report, it was Lady Mary Wortley Montagu who first drew attention to the waters themselves at Islington. She thought highly of them, but admitted that they made her sleepy if she drank too much. Mrs. Delany also referred approvingly to their rising fame. Perhaps the song written in 1733 and illustrated by George Bickham, writing-master and engraver, describes them best:

> *Behold the Walks, a chequer'd shade,*
> *In the gay pride of green array'd;*
> *How bright the sun! the air how still!*
> *In wild confusion there we view*
> *Red ribbons grouped with aprons blue;*
> *Scrapes, curtsies, nods, winks, smiles and frowns,*
> *Lords, milkmaids, duchesses and clowns,*
> *In their all-various dishabille.*

Despite her claim, Lady Mary Wortley Montagu was not the founder of Islington's prosperity as a watering-place. Like all the London spas, it had its ebbings and flowings of fortune. Even in 1714 *The Field Spy* said:

> *The ancient drooping trees unprun'd appear'd;*
> *No ladies to be seen; no fiddles heard.*

But it can hardly be disputed that its greatest prosperity came as the result of the visits of the princesses Amelia and Caroline, daughters of George II, in the May and June of 1733. Islington made the most of these occasions. Princess Amelia had not yet revealed in public the autocratic character that later was to make Londoners dislike her so much. Salutes of twenty-one guns greeted these royal young ladies, and it is said that as many as sixteen hundred people came out to see them in a single morning:

> *Of either sex whole droves together,*
> *To see and to be seen flocked thither,*
> *To drink—and not to drink—the water,*
> *And here promiscuously to chatter.*

Lodging houses sprang up overnight round the gardens, and from 1733 to 1770 Islington enjoyed a remarkable vogue, particularly among those with nothing better to do than talk scandal:

> *Lord! madam, did you e'er behold*
> *(Says one) a dress so very old?*
> *Sure that commode was made, i' faith,*
> *In days of Queen Elizabeth;*
> *At Charles the Second's coronation:*
> *The lady, by her mantua's forebody,*
> *Sure takes a pride to dress like nobody.*[1]

After 1770 its fortunes declined, though the gardens continued to be well cared for until the nineteenth century. By that time the region had become a well-to-do suburb; yet in 1776 we find George Colman in *The Spleen, or Islington Spa* writing: 'The Spa grows as genteel as Tonbridge, Brighthelmstone, Southampton or Margate ... Walks, balls, raffles and subscriptions ... and then Eliza's wedding, you know, was owing to the Spa. Oh! the watering-places are the only places to get young women lovers and husbands.' Even as late as 1826 a last attempt was made to revive Islington as a spa; but it had little success, and by the middle of the nineteenth century the growth of London had engulfed a large part of the gardens, at which the waters themselves, apparently, lost heart and ceased to flow.

Sadler's Wells (17), the other would-be rival of Tunbridge Wells, was separated by the still unburied Fleet from Islington, and here we have an instance—one of many as we shall see later—of a holy well becoming a place of entertainment. The original well belonged to St. John's Priory, Clerkenwell; but was buried after the dissolution until late in the seven-

[1] *Islington Walks, or the Threepenny Academy.*

16 'A New Song on Sadler's Wells,' 1728

From a song sheet engraved by G. Bickham

17 Sadler's Wells: the Aquatic Theatre, 1813

teenth century, when workmen employed by the unexpectedly immortalised Mr. Sadler, a surveyor of highways, accidentally uncovered it. While digging for gravel they struck a flat stone, which, when raised, proved to be supported by four oaken posts round a curiously carved well with a stone arch above it. Mr. Sadler lost no time in turning the discovery to profit when the waters were pronounced chalybeate. A fashionable doctor of the day named Morton, who suffered from ill-health, obligingly took a course of them and declared himself cured, whereupon Dr. Guidott, a recognised authority on mineral waters, described the case in a pamphlet. The water, he said, had 'a kind of ferruginous taste, somewhat like Tunbridge, but not altogether so strong of the steel, and having more of the nitrous sulphur flavour about it.' Prospective drinkers, to whom the word chalybeate may by this time have lost its first appeal, were further encouraged by Dr. Guidott's recommendation that caraways, or a glass of white or Rhenish wine should be taken with the waters. The obliging doctor even went so far as to say: 'it is very convenient for those who smoke tobacco, to take a pipe or two whilst their waters work.'

The gardens at Sadler's Wells were both less extensive and less attractive than those at Islington; but for a short time they might have up to six hundred visitors in a morning. When the well lost its appeal, as it soon did, a new attraction was provided in a music hall, and it was this rather than the spa that made the place popular—particularly when, in the sixteen-nineties, the entertainment side of the concern was taken over by James Miles, who was shortly afterwards joined by Francis Forcer the elder, a popular song writer of the day. In their time the spa was practically forgotten; but the music hall, according to the *Weekly Journal* of the 15th March 1718, became a rendezvous for 'strolling damsels, half-pay officers, peripatetic tradesmen, tars, butchers, and others that are musically inclined.' Rope-dancers and tumblers were introduced, and in *Humphry Clinker*, that classic of Spa literature, Elizabeth Jenkins describes the scene:

'I was afterwards of a party at Sadler's-wells, where I saw such tumbling and dancing upon ropes and wires, that I was frightened, and ready to go into a fit. I tho't it was all inchantment; and believing myself bewitched, began for to cry. You know as how the witches in Wales fly upon broomsticks; but here was flying without any broom-stick, or thing in the varsal world, and firing of pistols in the air, and blowing of trumpets, and swinging, and rolling of wheel-barrows upon a wire (God bless us!), no thicker than a sewing-threed; that, to be sure, they must deal with the devil.'

The gardens, however, were not entirely forsaken. Anglers in particular continued to use them, for as they were on the banks of the New River, which, incidentally, was not enclosed until 1862, they were better stocked with fish than the gardens along the Fleet can ever have been (17). It was, in fact, this ample supply of water available from the New River that enabled Sadler's Wells to stage the spectacular aquatic displays that were its greatest attractions during the eighteenth century. These were first shown in England in the old Sadler's Wells theatre, and were celebrated in the verse:

> Now the New River's current swells
> The reservoir of Sadler's Wells,
> And in some melodrame of slaughter
> Floats all the stage with real water.

The water for these displays was pumped up from the river into a well below the stage, and when the floor boards were taken up the audience saw a sheet of water, which might be used for setting off theatrical damsels, precariously seated on 'wooden rocks,' who would, on suitable occasions, be instructed to fall into the water in order to be rescued by their appointed swains. At other times famous naval battles could be presented here, or, at the other end of the dramatic scale, circus clowns could splash about to their hearts' content. The drenching act, still popular in circuses, was first performed at Sadler's Wells, where Joseph Grimaldi and Tom King—the original Sir Peter Teazle of *The School for Scandal*—made their names. Both were often as morose in private as they were cheerful in company. King ruined himself by gambling and died in poverty, while of Grimaldi the story is told that while delighting audiences with his merry capers he suffered from depression so acute that he consulted a doctor about it. The doctor laughed at his tale of misery: 'Go and see Grimaldi,' he said. 'I am Grimaldi,' replied the clown.

It is interesting to notice how often important shows at Sadler's Wells were advertised as being on nights of full-moon. The neighbourhood was then thought dangerous after nightfall. Sometimes horse patrols between the wells and the nearest streets were provided for patrons, while private parties would employ link-boys to light them home. Yet the fame of Sadler's Wells increased, and it was to the theatre not the spa that Fanny Burney's remark in *Evelina* applies: 'Pray, Cousin,' said Mr. Branghton, addressing the heroine, 'have you been at Sadler's Wells yet?' 'No, Sir.' 'No! why then you've seen nothing.'

If the entertaining aspects of spa life came late in London, the healing aspects came early. London may even have been preceded by Bath only—though Buxton might have a claim—among England's health resorts. And whether it qualifies for a place or not, there is certainly no other resort in England where the transformation of the holy wells of the Middle Ages into the spas of Caroline and Georgian England can be seen so clearly. In *Climates and Baths of Great Britain*, Dr. Norman Moore is quoted as saying that London may once have been 'a sanatorium for malarial cases from Essex.' He points out that after St. Erkenwald, bishop of the East Saxons and founder of Barking Abbey, was buried in his cathedral church of St. Paul, then the diocesan church of Essex, his tomb was visited regularly by pilgrims from the Essex marshes, who believed that if they could pray where their saint lay buried they would be healed. The litter in which he had been carried about when living remained in the church, and bits of its wood were chipped off because they were thought to ward off ague. It may well have been that these pilgrims were in fact cured, though by the air and water of Ludgate Hill and Clerkenwell rather than by the bishop's tomb or litter. Most of these London waters contained magnesium sulphate, or Epsom Salt, and were therefore useful as an aperient, though milder in their action than most of the purging waters in other parts of the country.

The patron saint of springs, St. Chad, was the brother of the most famous East Saxon bishop, St. Cedd, and this relationship would make the people of the eastern counties predisposed towards him from the beginning. It is therefore to be expected that several of the oldest wells in London and the Home Counties should be dedicated to him. The most frequented St. Chad's Well was on the east side of Gray's Inn Road, near King's Cross, and it is worth observing that the New River, which superseded the wells as the Londoners' most important water supply, rises from Chad's Well Springs in the meadows between Hertford and Ware. It was for this reason that the road it crossed on entering London was called Chadwell Lane.

St. Chad's Well, King's Cross, came into use as a spa in the seventeen-sixties, which was late. But late as this was, it remained popular for about sixty years, and preserved the traditions of the holy wells better than most of its neighbours in that it was always relatively respectable. Naturally, it had to exchange the patronage of a saint for the patronage of a physician, and in this case the doctor was as rude as the saint had been gentle. He was John Abernethy, who believed supremely in the remedial effects of purgative water and purgative speech. Seldom has a doctor been so cock-sure of himself, and apparently most of his patients took him at his own valuation. St. Chad, however, was not forgotten. He appeared as a rubicund figure in cloak and red nightcap in an oil painting hung in the pump-room, while another figure, called 'The Lady of the Well,' stood over the entrance to the gardens, with their clipped yews, box hedges, shady walks, and lawns with leaden statues, which attracted most of St. Chad's new votaries.

For a description of the original holy wells of London we turn to a history of the city written late in the twelfth century by William Fitz-Stephen, a monk of Canterbury, as preface to his life of St. Thomas à Becket. 'Round the city again,' he says, 'and towards the North arise certain excellent springs at a small distance, whose waters are sweet, salubrious, and clear, and whose runnels murmur o'er the shining stones: among these, Holywell [Shoreditch], Clerkenwell, and St Clement's Well may be esteemed the principal, as being much the most frequented, both by the scholars from the school [Westminster] and the youth from the city, when in a summer's evening they are disposed to take an airing.' Thus we see that already the holy wells of the city were being used as resorts and places where the more leisurely graces of life might be cultivated. But with the Reformation such interest as then survived in their sacred origin vanished, and by the time another century has passed most of the holy wells of London had become choked and forgotten. With the expansion of the city in the eighteenth century they were built over, so that it became impossible to trace them. Some, however, remained and were in use for household purposes until the middle of the nineteenth century, for it has to be remembered that in 1850 there were still eighty thousand houses in London without indoor water supply.

Of the three wells mentioned by FitzStephen, St. Clement's, near the Strand, was used until 1874. *The Times* for the 1st of May that year tells us that 'Another relic of Old London has lately passed away; the holy well of St. Clement, on the north of St. Clement Danes Church, has been filled in and covered over with earth and rubble, in order to form part of the Law Courts of the future.' Up to then there had been a pleasant green about the well, overlooked by Clement's Inn, and here, before the Reformation, Our Lord's Ascension was commemorated annually on Holy Thursday, or Ascension Day, when newly baptised converts used to parade in white robes, as doubtless they had done since the days when holy wells were used for the ceremony itself. An overflow from St. Clement's Well probably fed the Roman Spring Bath—or Plunge Bath—in Strand Lane, mentioned in *David Copperfield*.

FitzStephen's Holy Well in Shoreditch was choked up sometime during the eighteenth century. It was never a spa. But the Clerks-Well, which gave its name to Clerkenwell, *en* being an Anglo-Saxon plural ending, was at the heart of London's most popular group of spas (21). The reason for this was geological. The water that ran down from the heights in the north sank through the gravel, but was held up by the impervious London clay. In the broken, uneven land along the banks of the Fleet in this district, the accumulated water burst out in springs at various places. When John Stow was writing his *Survey of London* this was a residential suburb. He says: 'the fields here were commodious for the citizens to walk about and otherwise recruit their dulled spirits in the sweet and wholesome ayre.' Consequently 'many faire houses for gentlemen and others' had been built.

Like Skinners' Well near it, Clerks-Well illustrates the immemorial association of drama with wells, which George Bernard Shaw, normally regarded as an iconoclast, continued in our own day by having so many of his plays produced at Malvern. It was long the custom for the parish clerks of London, the acolytes of the Catholic priests, to perform miracle and mystery plays at Clerkenwell—the skinners at Skinners' Well—and no doubt these themselves succeeded pagan mummeries in the same open spaces. Clerkenwell had natural advantages that made it a favourite theatre for centuries. From Clerkenwell Green the land sloped down to the Fleet, forming a natural amphitheatre suitable for the purpose. Skinners' Well was equally favoured, and Stow tells us that in 1390 there was a play performed there, which 'continued three days together; the king, queen and nobles being present.' He relates also that in 1409 this was surpassed by a representation of the Creation that took eight days to perform and was attended by 'the most part of the nobles and gentles of England.'

Obviously there were many holy wells in London that never developed into spas and therefore do not come into the present survey—such as St. Bride's Well, situated near the palace of Bridewell, and Muswell, or Moss Well, said to have been visited by King John and still a place of pilgrimage in Mary's reign. Others besides those named by FitzStephen undoubtedly were holy wells before they became medicinal springs. St. Agnes-le-Clair's Bath, in Tabernacle Square, Finsbury, was a notable example. Roman coins were found there in the eighteenth century, and an advertisement in 1756 describes the bath as 'much applauded by the learned physicians of old, and now greatly extolled by the most eminent professors of this age.' A curious dialogue between a country gentleman and a citizen in *The Pleasant Walks of Moore Fields* (1607) gives a popular legend of the well's origin:

'COUNTRY GENT. But, Sir, here are stones set upright; what is the meaning of them?

'CITIZEN. Marry! where they stand runs a Spring called Dame Annis le Cleare, after the name of a rich London Widow, Annis Clare, who, matching herself with a riotous Courtier in the time of Edward I, he vainly consumed all her wealth: there she drowned herself, being then but a shallow ditch of running water.'

The spring here is said to have flowed at the rate of ten thousand gallons a day, so it was possible to use its water for a fairly considerable bathing establishment, which evidently had pleasure gardens attached, for in 1748 the proprietor complained that rock-work, artificial fruit-trees, and two glass swans had been stolen from a fountain in the grounds.

Some of the holy wells lost their original names at the Reformation, when what had formerly been revered came to be derided. Bagnigge Wells is an instance. This, like several others, was on the banks of the Fleet, sometimes called The River of Wells. It is now lost under King's Cross Station, just as St. Pancras's Well, which flourished in the eighteenth century, is lost under the neighbouring station. Indeed the railways seem to have displaced the spas in this part of London, for the Metropolitan Railway runs down the old channel of the Fleet along Farringdon Road. The appearance of this part of London was very different when Bagnigge Wells flourished and the Fleet was a pretty stream, still open and unpolluted. From its gardens on the slope of Pentonville, visitors could look out towards the breezy heights of Primrose Hill, Hampstead, and Islington. And so rural was the countryside about St. Pancras that when the Elizabethan Nash greeted Kempe, the comedian, he exclaimed: 'As many Allhailes to thy person as there be haicockes in July at Pancredge.' Pepys, it will be recalled, took a trip out to St. Pancras one Sunday. 'After dinner,' he wrote on the 23rd April 1665, 'Creed and we by Coach took the ayre in the fields beyond St. Pancras, it raining now and then, which it seems is most welcome weather.' The gardens were laid out in walks through shady avenues of trees along the south slope of Church Hill, and were so extensive that cows were kept 'to accommodate ladies and gentlemen with new milk and cream and syllabubs in the greatest perfection,' while the waters from the well were reputed to be a powerful antidote against 'rising of the vapours,' stone, gravel, and as 'a general and sovereign help to nature.'

Bagnigge Wells (19) are thought to have belonged to the Benedictine Nunnery of St. Mary's, Clerkenwell, and to have been known as Blessed Mary's Well. A popular story relates that after the Reformation 'Blessed Mary' became 'Black Mary,' but this is disputed by some authorities, who say that Black Mary was a coloured woman named Mary Wollaston, who attended at another well nearby. The origin of the name Bagnigge is clear enough: it was the name of a person living at the spa house when the medicinal properties of the well were discovered. Perhaps the most suitable name would have been 'Nell Gwyn's Well,' for in its heyday she was certainly its governing spirit. According to a tradition which, while it cannot be proved authentic, appears to be better founded than most of its kind, the spa house was Nell's country home for a time.

Though the house had previously been a place of public entertainment, the discovery that the water from two old wells in its garden were medicinal was not made until 1757, when a Mr. Hughes, the tenant at the time, used them for watering his plants, which promptly wilted and almost died. Surprised at this strange reaction, Mr. Hughes invited Dr. Bevis, a well-known physician and astronomer of the day, to analyse the water of both wells separately, and it was found that one had 'an agreeable sub-acid tartness' similar to that of the German chalybeates, the other cathartic properties which made it a powerful purgative. In 1760 Dr. Bevis published his findings and recommended the waters to all and sundry. But Mr. Hughes had already thrown his gardens open to the public. In 1759 the *Public Advertiser* announced:

'Bagnigge Wells are now open for the reception of company, both the chalybeate and purging waters being in the greatest perfection. Proper conveniency and attendance, breakfasting, etc.—N.B. Three half-pints of the purging water is sufficient for most people.—No Salts are required to quicken their virtue.'

The two wells in the Bagnigge gardens were forty feet apart; but their water was piped to a 'temple,' a circular colonnade supporting a dome, the whole surrounded by a low balustrade. Within stood the pump, which had two spouts, one delivering chalybeate, the other cathartic water. Of the immediate popularity of Bagnigge there can be no doubt whatever. Its name constantly reappears in the minor literature of the day. In *The Shrubs of Parnassus* (1760) we find the lines:

> . . . *there stands a dome superb,*
> *Hight Bagnigge, where, from our forefathers hid,*
> *Long have two springs in dull stagnation slept.*

A later owner developed the amenities of the gardens until they became, perhaps, the most frequented resort within easy reach of the city. Hundreds of people came out each morning to drink the waters and stroll about in the gardens, pausing by the pond to watch the goldfish, then a novelty in England, and to gaze in wonder at the fountain, an artificial swan with a Dutch cupid astride its back, which stood in the centre and spouted water into the air through its beak, to the great delight of children. In the afternoons a different crowd came out, this time for tea and muffins in the long-room, or in one of the arbours romantically smothered with sweet-briar and honeysuckle, which were placed at intervals all the way round the gardens. In the evenings, couples would stroll along the formal walks bordered with holly and box, admire the 'rural' cottage, cross one of the three bridges that spanned the stream and visit the 'grotto,' a castellated building, hexagonal in shape and large enough to hold nearly twenty people. The walls were adorned in the manner of the time with coloured pebbles, glass, and pretty shells. Two tall leaden figures completed the most admired features of this London arcady, one a Ganymede wielding a scythe, the other a Phyllis holding a rake as becomingly as if it were a parasol. Along the banks of the Fleet, seats were provided. Some of the visitors fished, while others, more energetically inclined, turned to the bowling or the skittle alleys. Only on the seats by the river bank were smoking and the drinking of ale or cider permitted.

From a poem attributed to Charles Churchill, entitled *Bagnigge Wells, a poem, in which are portrayed the characters of the most eminent filles de joye, with Notes illustrative, critical, historical, and explanatory,* we get an idea of the character of the place in such lines as:

> *Thy arbours, Bagnigge, and the gay alcove*
> *Where frail nymphs in amorous dalliance rove,*
> *Where 'Prentice youths enjoy the Sunday feast,*
> *And City matrons boast their Sabbath best,*
> *Where unfledged Templars first as fops parade,*
> *And new made ensigns sport their first cockade.*

The Shrubs of Parnassus has a similar account of the company:

> *Here ambulates th' Attorney, looking grave,*
> *And Rake, from Bacchanalian rout uprose,*
> *And mad festivity. Here, too, the Cit,*
> *With belly turtle-tufted, and Man of Gout*
> *With leg of size enormous. Hobbling on,*
> *The pump-room he salutes, and in the chair*
> *He squats himself unwieldy. Much he drinks,*
> *And much he laughs, to see the females quaff*
> *The friendly beverage.*

By the middle of the eighteenth century all the English spas had many features in common: formal gardens, pump-room, long-room—where tea was served with cakes and syllabubs—and entertainment room, the pavilion

18 Islington Spa, about 1730

From a song sheet engraved by G. Bickham, 1733

19 The Company at Bagnigge Wells, 1772

of the provincial spas. The long-room at Bagnigge Wells was an apartment of some dignity. It had been the banqueting hall of the original Bagnigge House, and in it Nell Gwyn's bust was accorded the place of honour. But the place as a whole lost its early superior character and came to be patronised only by the rowdier Londoners—Smithfield butchers, Turnmill Street knackers, who enjoyed the dog-fights and pugilistic encounters that displaced the earlier and more elegant entertainments, particularly after threepenny concerts had been introduced. The end of Bagnigge was in sight when this stage was reached. Gradually, as the new music-halls sprang up all round the gardens, competition became keener and the popularity of the gardens waned. One lessee succeeded another; but none was able to save the place, and in 1842 the gardens went out of use. London streets crept over them, until all that remained of the glories of Bagnigge Wells was a public house bearing their name.

Within a mile of St. Pancras and Bagnigge Wells, all in the gay London fields described by Ben Jonson in *A Tale of a Tub*, there were six other medicinal springs with gardens laid out in similar fashion. There was Powis Well behind Powis House in Lamb's Conduit Fields, close to the Foundling Hospital. For news of this we turn again to the advertisement columns of contemporary newspapers. In one of these, dated 4th August 1748, we learn that its long-room was to be opened the following Monday with an assembly of country dancing. From another newspaper advertisement we learn that its waters 'are recommended by many eminent Physicians and Surgeons for the cure of breakings out, sore legs, inflammation of the eyes, and other scorbutic disorders, &c.'

At another of these six springs, London Spaw, the home-brewed ale appears to have been in greater demand than the water. An advertisement of 1754 informs the public that 'during the time of the Welsh Fair, held in the Spa Field, will be the usual entertainment of roast pork, with the oft-famed flavoured Spaw Ale.' (Spaw, it may be observed in passing, was Dr. Johnson's spelling and pronunciation of the word). There was never any justification for the pretentious name of this particular well. It was always a minor spa, but in a description of the gardens in *May-day, or the Origin of Garlands* (1720), it is shown to have had the normal attractions:

> *Now ninepin alleys and now skittles grace*
> *The late forlorn, sad, desolate place;*
> *Arbours of jasmine, fragrant shades compose,*
> *And numerous blended companies enclose.*
> *The spring is gratefully adorn'd with rails,*
> *Whose fame shall last till the New River fails!*

Nowhere else in London were spas so numerous. But there were others. Pepys visited Marylebone Gardens (20), on the east side of Marylebone High Street, and found it 'a pretty place.' The spring here was not discovered until the winter of 1773-4, by which time music-halls offered greater attractions than spas, and all the fancied ailments requiring water treatment were forgotten for a time. A music-hall was established at Marylebone, and this, along with the gardens, attracted visitors for a few years. The waters were never in much demand, and the normal order of spa life was reversed here in that when the patients went out the doctors came in, for when Devonshire Place, parts of Upper Wimpole Street and Devonshire Street were built over the spa gardens, the new residences were taken at once by the most distinguished physicians of the day.

As London society became more refined the old spa gardens were replaced by tea-gardens, which in turn gave place to our modern parks. Regent's Park, formerly Marylebone Park, adjoins the site of Marylebone Gardens, while Hyde Park and Kensington Gardens are on the site of the Kensington springs. The two in Hyde Park have gone; but the one in Kensington Gardens, to the south of the Round Pond, remains. Its name, St. Govor's Well, does not indicate that it is an ancient holy well. The name was given to it as a compliment to Lord Llanover, who as Sir Benjamin Hall was First Commissioner of Works for three years from 1855, and took his title from Llanover, near Abergavenny, so called from its association with this particular saint.

There were several spas south of the Thames, but most of them belong to a period later than that of the spas proper. The name is applied to these only because it was still retained by their older counterparts north of the river, which by this time had become places of entertainment and little more. Several, however, must be mentioned, if only for their pleasant associations with the great. Bermondsey, on the bank of the Neckinger, was the most important. The owner of the gardens when the spring was discovered in 1770 was Thomes Keyse, the artist, who made use of them for displaying his paintings, and exercised his talent to good effect in furnishing and decorating the music-room. Finch's Grotto Gardens and the Restoration Spring Gardens were in the same class, and all three enjoyed several years of popularity in the last quarter of the seventeenth century. Lambeth Wells and St. George's Spa were genuine spas—that is to say, their waters had mineral properties and were taken medicinally. The two purging springs at Lambeth were in Lambeth Walk, where 'The Fountain' inn stood later, now converted into Messrs. Body's outfitters' shop, or No. 105. They came into fashion late in the seventeenth century. A house, surmounted by a gilded ball, was built over them, and the assembly-room was known, according to an advertisement of 1721, for its 'consorts of very good music, with French and country dancing.'

Within half a mile of Lambeth Wells, in fields where Gerard collected specimens for his *Herball*, was a well that had the distinction of being recommended by another great collector of plants, Dr. John Fothergill, who said that its waters would 'cure most cutaneous disorders, and be useful for keeping the body cool, and preventing cancerous affections,' As the result of this professional puff, the spa prospered, and in 1731 the old 'Dog and Duck,' as it had been called, was enobled by the title of St. George's Spa. Forty years later Mrs. Thrale, on the advice of Dr. Johnson, drank the waters, and it would be interesting to know whether this had any connection with Mrs. Thrale's state of expectancy that summer. It was about this time that Johnson wrote to his friend, Bennet Langton: 'The Queen and Mrs. Thrale, both ladies of experience, yet both missed their reckoning this summer.' Perhaps it would be unwise to speculate on this, for as the doctor remarked in the same letter: 'Ladies will have these tricks.'

Chapter Four

LONDON'S COUNTRY WELLS

You ask me where in peaceful grot,
I'd choose to fix my dwelling.
I'll tell you! for I've found the spot,
And mortals call it Welwyn.

THEODORE HOOK

I. NORTH OF THE THAMES

WHEN, on the 11th July 1664, Pepys wrote: 'I and my man Will on horseback by my wife to Barnet; a very pleasant day,' he gave us a clue to the brief but considerable popularity of London's country wells. To the townsman, a day in the country, without more than the small degree of discomfort that gave it piquancy, had recently—and only recently—become attractive. It was the new fashion to construct rustic arbours and thatched retreats in town gardens in order to produce an illusion of rusticity; but how much better to ride out ten or twenty miles into Surrey, Kent, Essex, or Hertfordshire—into Middlesex even—and find the authentic scene! In Pepys's day the roads were still so rough that it was impossible for anyone to travel more than a few miles even in the length of a midsummer day. But gradually the water-drinkers were becoming bolder and more adventurous. From Clerkenwell and Islington they climbed the hill to Hampstead, or invaded Kilburn. If the weather permitted and the daylight was long enough they might go on to Muswell Hill, Totteridge, Northaw, Barnet, or even Welwyn. Hackney, Tottenham, Woodford, and Chigwell attracted those on the east of the city; Acton those on the west; while south of the Thames, as the other great diarist of the day, Evelyn, discovered, another galaxy of springs threw up their sparkling waters to regale fair and gallant visitors to Camberwell, Dulwich, Streatham, Sydenham, Beulah, or Carshalton; to Richmond or Cobham on the west; and to Shooter's Hill on the east.

The Barnet waters, which were among the strongest, were not altogether to Pepys's taste: 'I and Will to see the Wells,' he continues, 'and there I drunk three glasses, and walked, and come back and drunk two more; and

44

so we rode home, round by Kingsland, Hackney, and Mile End, till we were quite weary.' That night he slept little. 'About eleven o'clock, knowing what money I have in the house, and hearing a noise, I began to sweat worse and worse, till I melted almost to water . . . it was only the dog.'

This was not Pepys's only visit to the mineral spring at Barnet, which sprang from the common nearly a mile west of the town. It had first been advertised in the *Perfect Diurnal* of the 5th June 1652,[1] and by 1660 was so popular that in Dr. Wittie's *Scarborough Spaw* it is mentioned along with Epsom, Tunbridge, and Harrogate:

> Let Epsom, Tunbridge, Barnet, Knaresborough be
> In what request they will, Scarborough for me.

On the 11th of August 1667—again in midsummer—Pepys paid his second visit. He rose early one 'Lord's Day' morning and was at Barnet by seven o'clock. There were already many at the well besides himself, so after drinking three glasses he went into the town, and at the 'Red Lion,' his usual inn, had some of the landlord's noted cheese cakes, which, he said, were among the best he had ever eaten.

Fuller tells us in the *Worthies* that even in 1660 'the catalogue of the cures done by this spring amounteth to a great number; insomuch that there is hope, in process of time, the water rising here will repair the blood shed hard by, and save as many lives as were lost in the fatal battle of Barnet.' All the eighteenth-century writers on Hertfordshire sang its praises, and as late as 1800 a pamphlet, entitled *The Barnet Well Water*, was published by the Rev. W. M. Trinder, M.D. Forty years later a farmhouse had replaced the Well House, and the well itself had been enclosed.

Celia Fiennes was another early visitor to Barnet, and it is from her that we have the best description. She tells us that the well was enclosed in a building, similar in design to the modern building that now covers the original basins, with lattices of wood, through which spectators could see the water. Those who wished to drink had to descend steps. Celia went down them, but did not drink. She found the water so deep that she could not see the bottom. It was full of leaves and dirty, and when drawn from the well it had to stand for a few minutes to give the sediment time to settle. It then became clear enough; but she had no stomach for it, preferring the wells with stone basins, like those at Tunbridge and Hampstead, where she could actually see the springs bubble up out of the ground, and therefore knew that the water was fresh. The old well-room, with the steps used by the fashionable people of London in the seventeenth and eighteenth

[1] H. B. Wheatley, *Diary of Pepys*, vol. iv, p. 179, footnote.

centuries, was accidentally discovered in the present century, and is now carefully preserved in an open space at the centre of the Well House Estate where, by a happy thought, the names of Well Road, Trinder Road, and Pepys Crescent have been given to modern roads.

Both Kilburn and Muswell Hill spas were secularised holy wells. The Kilburn spring was near the site of an Augustinian nunnery suppressed in 1536. About the middle of the eighteenth century its long-room opened for music, dancing, and various other entertainments, and continued to attract day-trippers from London until about 1830. Goldsmith, who seems to have enjoyed strolling through the London pleasure gardens, is said to have been fond of Kilburn, and even to have written part of the *Deserted Village* and *She Stoops to Conquer* there. The association is perpetuated in the name, Goldsmith's Place. But Goldsmith's most familiar description of the typical tea-garden scene is of the White Conduit House near the present King's Cross Station. 'Here the inhabitants often assemble,' he says, 'to celebrate a feast of hot rolls and butter.' Washington Irving has an amusing story of Goldsmith escorting three young ladies of his acquaintance into the gardens of the White Conduit House and entertaining them in his usual expansive manner. But when the waiter came round with the reckoning poor Noll fumbled uncomfortably in his pockets for a few minutes, searching for the coins that were seldom there, until a friend, observing his plight, came to his rescue and allowed the impecunious poet to retire with dignity.

The Muswell Hill spring had been known for its cures since the eleventh century at the latest. In 1112 a chapel, long known as the chapel of Our Lady of Muswell, was built over it by monks of the Priory of St. John of Jerusalem, Clerkenwell, to whom the land had been given by the Bishop of London, lord of the manor of Hornsea. After the suppression it passed to the Cowper family, and eventually came to the Roes, one of whom built there 'a faire house.' Weever, in his *Ancient Funeral Monuments* (1631), says that the well was in Sir Nicholas Roe's cellar, adding: 'Here was sometime an Image of Our Lady of Muswell, whereunto was a continuall resort, in the way of pilgrimage, growing (as it goes by tradition from father to the sonne) in regard of a great cure which was performed by this water upon a King of Scots, who being strangely diseased, was (by some divine intelligence) advised to take the water of a Well in England; which, after long scrutation and inquisition, this Well was found, and performed the cure.'

It was another King of Scots, James, sixth of Scotland and first of England, who brought fame to the Northaw spring, which was actually at Lower Cuffley, between Northaw and Cheshunt, at the point marked 'King's

Well' on the Ordnance Survey map. It became a place of resort with the courtiers when the king was in residence at his palace of Theobalds nearby, and on September 11th 1660 Charles II gave permission for it to be called The King's Well.[1] But the Northaw, or Cuffley, spa has long been forgotten except by a few of the older people in the neighbourhood, who remember that it was of no use for brewing tea. Though naturally colourless, the water turned a nasty inky colour when boiled and poured on the tea, from the combination of the iron in the water and the tannin in the tea. Charles Lamb, in a letter to Charles Cowden Clarke, December 1828, refers to a well at Northaw dedicated to St. Claridge, which was surrounded by clumps of moss known to the natives as 'Claridge's covers.' According to a legend recorded, Lamb tells us, in the *Black Book of St. Albans*, the saint entertained angels and hermits at the well on the occasion of the blessing of the waters, and these clumps were the cushions they sat on.

Welwyn and Totteridge, two other spas north of London, were never considerable. Welwyn owed what little fame it enjoyed to the interest of its rector, Dr. Young, author of *Night Thoughts*, whom we met at Tunbridge Wells. Dr. Young was rector of Welwyn for twenty-five years, and his tomb is to be seen in the chancel of his old church. Dr. Johnson, it may be recalled, visited the poet's son at Welwyn in 1781, and Boswell records the scene: 'Sir,' said Johnson, with a very polite bow, 'I had a curiosity to come and see this place. I had the honour to know that great man, your father.' In the garden they were shown 'a gravel walk, on each side of which was a row of trees, planted by Dr. Young, which formed a handsome Gothic arch; Dr. Johnson called it a fine grove.'

But Barnet, Kilburn, Muswell Hill, and the rest of this northern group, with one exception, were but small concerns. The one important London spa to the north of the cockney wells already considered was Hampstead which, unlike Islington and Sadler's Wells, really did mean to London what Tunbridge Wells meant, though on a less ambitious scale. What Hampstead was to the England of Queen Anne we may read in the comedy *Hampstead Heath*, produced at Drury Lane in 1706:

'SMART. HAMPSTEAD for awhile assumes the day; the lovely season of the year, the shining crowd assembled at this time, and the noble situation of the place, gives us the nearest show of Paradise.

'BLOOM. London now indeed has but a melancholy aspect, and a sweet rural spot seems an adjournment o' the nation, where business is laid fast asleep, variety of diversions feast our fickle fancies, and every man wears a face of pleasure. The cards fly, the bowl runs, the dice rattle . . . '

[1] Clutterbuck, *History of the County of Hertford* (1821), vol. ii, p. 411.

'SMART. Assemblies so near the town give us a sample of each degree. We have court ladies that are all air and no dress; city ladies that are over-dressed and no air; and country dames with brown faces like a Stepney bun; besides an endless number of Fleet Street sempstresses, that...'

'ARABELLA. Well, this Hampstead's a charming place—to dance all night at the Wells, and be treated at Mother Huff's—to have presents made at one at the Raffling-shops, and then take a walk in Cane Wood with a man of wit that's not over rude—'[1]

The first known reference to Hampstead as a spa was in Charles II's reign, but there was no development until, in 1698, the spring, with six acres of land round it, was presented to the poor of the parish by the Countess of Gainsborough and her son. Two years later the waters were first advertised, and about the same time they were actually bottled and sold at the 'Eagle and Child' in Fleet street at threepence a flask. A Dr. Gibbons came forward to pronounce them 'not inferior to any of our chalybeate springs, and coming very near Pyrmont in quality.' With such medical support as this, all that Hampstead required to make it yet another resort of the rich, the idle, and the vain, were those facilities for outdoor and indoor amusement that quickly took shape in long-room, assembly-room, concert-room, bowling green, race-course, and even a church, which, like those of other spas, had about as much to do with religion as the waters had to do with healing. Indeed, the Hampstead chapel later acquired a notoriety for the solemnisation of irregular marriages comparable with that of Keith's Chapel in Mayfair, in spite of its Puritan name of Sion. In 1716 an advertisement appeared in *Read's Weekly Journal*, informing the public that 'Sion Chapel, at Hampstead, being a private and pleasure place, many persons of the best fashion have lately been married there. Now as a minister is obliged constantly to attend, this is to give Notice, that all persons upon bringing a Licence, and who shall have their Wedding Dinner in the Gardens, may be married in that said Chapel, *without giving any fee or reward whatsoever:* and such as do not keep their Wedding Dinner at the Gardens, only Five Shillings will be demanded of them for all fees.' Nor was that the first such advertisement. The earliest one known is said to be dated April 1710. So the custom was evidently well established at Hampstead, and these 'Fleet Marriages,' as they are commonly called, were arranged by proprietors of the various houses of entertainment as part of the local amenities.

In spite of what Dr. Gibbons said about them, the waters were not

[1] Park's *Hampstead*, pp. 242-5.

20 MARYLEBONE GARDENS. 'A View of the Orchestra, with the Band of Music, in the Grand Walk'

From a print by J. Donowell, 1761

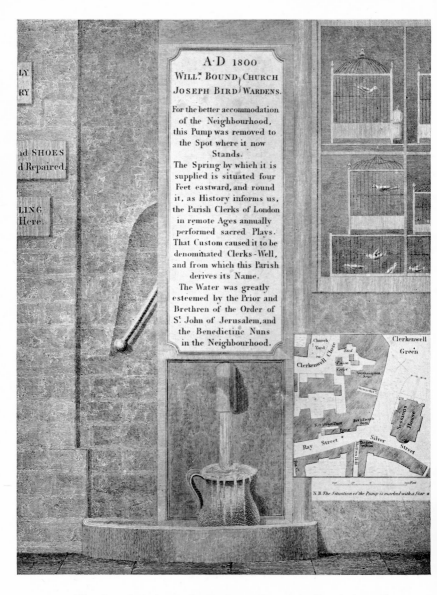

21 The site of Clerks-Well (Clerkenwell), originally a holy well,
as it appeared in 1822

From a contemporary print

important; but Hampstead, with its bracing atmosphere, breezy heath and pleasant groves had advantages not easily matched by its neighbours, and its history—particularly it cultural history—gives it a notable place in an account of the English spas. It was, perhaps, fortunate that the town did not have to depend for its livelihood on the waters, though the prudent doctors were careful to cover their inadequacy with fine, or perhaps we should say florid, language. One account of them declared that they were 'a stimulant diuretic, very beneficial in chronic diseases arising from languor of the circulation, general debility of the system, or laxity of the solids, or in all cases where tonics and gentle stimulants are required.' This, as Walford the antiquary remarked, amounted to saying that they were good for persons 'whose principal complaints were those of idleness, dissipation, and frivolity.'

Hampstead's reign of fashion lasted only about twenty years; but during that time wits were attracted as well as dandies. It was the summer head-quarters of the Kit-Cat Club, who met in rooms at the Upper Flask Tavern, where Swift, Addison, and Steele were often to be met in company with Dr. Arbuthnot, the Queen's physician. The Flask succeeded the Wells, an older house of entertainment, as the resort of Hampstead's élite. Another house, called the Wells Hotel, has replaced the original Wells Tavern. The first house had more extensive grounds, as we may see from a decree of the Court of Chancery, to whom the property fell in 1719. According to this there was a 'tavern, coffee-room, dancing-room, raffling-shops, bowling green.' In the *Tatler*, No. 50, Hampstead's raffling-shop is said to have been set up by a lawyer as an 'easier way of conveyancing and alienating estates from one family to another,' which may explain how the Wells Tavern got into the hands of the Court of Chancery. Its long-room, which stood where Wells House stands now, was for some time the headquarters of the Hampstead (3rd Middlesex) Volunteers. It was then converted into a chapel and served the local Presbyterians until the present Church in High Street was built in 1861-2. Seldom can a building have witnessed such varied scenes. The spiritual gulf between St. Chad and The Lady of the Well at St. Chad's Well, King's Cross, seems almost harmony when compared with that between the elders of the kirk and the Nine Muses, whose figures were found on the walls of the chapel when the superimposed colouring was washed off by the Volunteers. The site of the pump-room is now occupied by Wellside, a private house overlooking the Gainsborough Gardens. These gardens were formerly a pond, and we can imagine how pleasant it would be to sit by the old pump-room windows and look out on the water, with the great branches of the chestnut tree drawn down to touch it.

4**

Brief as Hampstead's fame as a watering-place in the literal sense was, it continued to attract the well-to-do as a place of residence, and to maintain its associations with men of letters. The site of the spring is preserved by a stone fountain in Well Walk, opposite Constable's house, but the water supply was cut off several years ago. So Hampstead is no longer a spa. It is now visited not for its waters, but for the sake of the poet, John Keats, who lived in Keats Grove in 1817-18, while writing *Endymion*. Often as he sat on his favourite seat here he must have thought of the members of the Kit-Cat Club,

> *Or when, Apollo-like, thou'rt pleas'd to lead*
> *Thy sons to feast on Hampstead's airy mead,*
> *Hampstead, that towering in superior sky*
> *Now with Parnassus does in honour vie.*[1]

He must also have thought of the flight of Clarissa Harlowe to the Upper Flask, as Richardson tells the story, of Evelina's visit to the Hampstead tea-gardens in 1778, and of the many other shades that flit through these walks in the minds of bookmen—shades that he was prematurely to join. But the heath takes a ray of light from his own three lines in *Endymion*,

> *. . . where sweet air stirs*
> *Blue hare-bells lightly, and where prickly furze*
> *Buds lavish gold . . .*

Acton, to the west of this northern group, had purging waters that attracted visitors for a short time, and were very necessary in those days of over-eating. Three springs in the gardens at Acton Wells House at the south-west corner of the Old Oak Common, near Wormwood Scrubs, were advertised in Queen Anne's reign, and Lysons, writing in 1795, says of them that their water was impregnated with calcareous glauber salt second only to Cheltenham's in potency. They appear to have continued in fashion longer than most of those already mentioned, for in 1771 an advertisement stated that 'By the recommendation of Physicians and the encouragement of the nobility and gentry Acton Wells are newly opened for the benefit of the public. Every Monday, Wednesday and Friday from Lady Day to Michaelmas, are public days for drinking the waters and breakfasting.' The water, like that from other wells in the Home Counties, was sold at 'Mr. Owen's original mineral water warehouse in Fleet Street.'

The eastern group began at Hackney with springs on the downs, and found a patron saint at Tottenham, where St. Eloy's Well and Bishop's

[1] Sir Richard Blackmore, *The Kit-Cats, a Poem*, 1708.

Well were in high repute for the purity of their water. On the western edge of the parish there was a well dedicated to St. Dunstan. These have been swept away by the tide of London streets that now cover them. But north-east of them, in the ancient Forest of Waltham, now surviving in Epping and Hainault forests, Woodford Wells and Chigwell preserve in their names, if in little else, the memory of wells that were spas for a short time at the beginning of the eighteenth century.

Little is known about the Woodford wells. There were several of them. The Essex historian, Philip Morant, writing in 1768, says: 'Woodford Wells were formerly in repute as purgative and good for many illnesses.' Like Barnet, Woodford was an easy ride from the city, and what could have been pleasanter than a stroll on the green, with its wide prospects across the Roding valley, after breakfasting, in the manner of the day, on almond cheese cakes, tarts, seed or plum cakes, baked with fresh Epping butter? The most important well was near the inn called the 'Horse and Groom,' which in consequence became the 'Horse and Well.' It is now at the rear of a weather-boarded shop nearby. Hood's reference to 'the Wells' in his rollicking *Epping Hunt* is to the inn, not the spring:

> Now many a sign at Woodford Town
> Its Inn-vitation tells;
> But Huggins, full of ills, of course,
> Betook him to the Wells.

Lysons describes this well as being 'near the nine-mile stone, in the Forest.' It is on high ground, and springs from a bank of gravel between the Roding and the Ching. The well at Chigwell Row, now lost, described as being 'behind the windmill, among the trees,' was warmly praised by a Dr. Frewin, a native of the parish, who returned regularly to drink the water. Apparently it enabled him to survive three wives.

The one well in this forest neighbourhood that did bid fair to becoming an important spa was at Wanstead. It was close to the Blake Hall Road, and though a fountain was put up near the site, and serves to mark the spot, this never supplied water from the original well, which gave out as the result of draining operations in the vicinity. It was probably the inadequacy of the water supply that prevented Wanstead, then a fashionable village, with everything else in its favour, from developing into another Hampstead or Tunbridge even, particularly as it was one of the first in the field. John Chamberlain, the letter writer, wrote to Sir Dudley Carleton on the 23rd August 1619[1]: 'We have great noise here of a new Spa, or spring of that

[1] State Papers Dom. James I, CX., No. 26.

nature, found lately about Wanstead; and much running there is to it daily, both by lords and ladies and other great company, so that they have almost drawn it dry already; and, if it should hold on, it would put down the waters at Tunbridge; which, for these three or four years, have been much frequented, specially this summer, by many great persons; insomuch that they that have seen both say that it [*i.e.* Tunbridge] is not inferior to the Spa [in Belgium] for good company, numbers of people, and other appurtenances.'

II. SOUTH OF THE THAMES

As we had Pepys to introduce us to the country wells north of the Thames, we may consider ourselves doubly honoured in having Evelyn to introduce us to those on the south. He drank the Shooter's Hill waters in August 1699, and nearly two hundred years later, in 1884, Walford, in his *Greater London,* says that the most popular of the Shooter's Hill Wells, which was then in a garden behind the Royal Military Academy, was still used. But the important central group south of the river began with Camberwell (23), where Evelyn visited Sir Edmund Bowyer in 1657 and thought his house a 'melancholie seat.' The odd thing about Camberwell in the history of the spas is that it actually produced a new one in the present century. In 1906, as reported in the *Daily Telegraph* for the 5th of June that year, bathers using the new public baths in the Old Kent Road complained that the water was always dirty. After analysing it, Dr. Bousfield declared that this much maligned water was, in fact, 'unusually rich in iron, being comparable in this respect with the Tunbridge Wells water, and it would appear almost as if the Council were in the position to set up a spa in the Old Kent Road.'

Dulwich, to the south of Camberwell, though its name appears earlier, did not become a spa till the middle of the eighteenth century. The principal well was at the junction of Lordship Lane with Dulwich Common Lane, approximately one mile south-east of Dulwich College. At the time of its discovery, this well was behind the Green Man Tavern, and was discovered while digging for household water. Professor John Martyn, F.R.S., was standing by at the time, and when the water broke through he tasted it and realised that here was a new medicinal spring. The result of his analysis was communicated to the Philosophical Transactions of the Royal Society. With such an asset in its garden, the name of the tavern was promptly changed to 'Dulwich Wells,' and the waters were not only sold on the spot, but were supplied regularly to St. Bartholomew's Hospital.

For forty years the success of the spa continued. In 1762, and doubtless in other years, its 'Great Breakfast Room' was advertised, and its waters were drunk until, towards the end of the century, the demand fell off and the tavern became a private house called 'Dulwich Grove.' Lord Chancellor Thurlow occupied it for a short time. It then became a school, kept by a Dr. Glennie, who had Byron as a pupil from 1799 to 1901. Two houses have occupied the site since then. The present one is called the Grove Hotel, but no trace remains of Professor Martyn's new spa.

Dulwich and its neighbour, Sydenham, were often confused; but we can always tell which is meant by glancing at the date of the reference. Those earlier than 1739 are to Sydenham, so when Culpepper tells us that the Juniper 'grows plentifully hard by the New-found Wells at Dulwich,' we know that Sydenham is meant. Discovered on Sydenham Common in 1640, the old doggerel says of it:

> And there you will find a wild rural retreat,
> From time immemorial called Sydenham Wells,
> With old Betty Evans, complacent and neat,
> And a Gypsy, if wished, who your fortune foretells.

Evelyn was here on the 2nd September 1675 after a visit to Dulwich College. 'Came back by certain medicinal Spa waters,' he wrote, 'at a place called Sydnam Wells, in Lewisham parish, much frequented in summer.' He returned in 1677. Evidently the well became popular about the middle of the seventeenth century; but as it had neither long-room, music-room, nor any of the amenities provided at the fashionable spas, it was little used except by the poor, who flocked to it every week-end. The well house itself was never more than a cottage, and as those who came to Sydenham for treatment had to lodge in huts on the common, the place was looked at askance by the proud and self-consciously respectable—not, perhaps, without reason. Of the week-end scene a well-known doctor of the day wrote: 'I cannot omit to take notice of a very great abuse occasioned by a rabble of Londoners and others frequenting these wells on Sundays, where, under pretence of drinking of the waters, they spend that holy day in great profaneness: who after they have gorged themselves with the water, do drink upon it an excessive quantity of Brandy (that Bane of Englishmen), thereby many of them becoming greatly prejudiced in their health (to add to their folly and crime) have not been ashamed to impute their indisposition to this Water.'

In spite of its rather disreputable character, Sydenham boasted a royal visitor in the person of George III, who came to the well cottage and spent several hours in conversation with the old woman who lived there, while his escort of Life Guards attracted considerable attention outside.

One thing worth noting about Sydenham, because we shall find similar phenomena elsewhere, is recorded by a Dr. John Peter, who praised the well in florid language in 1680. 'It is observable,' he says, 'that in that very place where now the Wells are, there used to be only gushings of waters, where multitudes of pigeons used to frequent; enough to give intelligence to any observing naturalist that there was something wherewith the water was impregnated that did invite and delight them, some saline aluminous liquor, of which the fowls naturally love to be tippling.'

When the spa declined, the well-house was taken over by St. George's Bowmen, a society of archers founded in 1789, who used it as their headquarters, the common being a convenient practice-ground until most of it was enclosed after the passing of the General Enclosure Act in 1801. Wells Road now covers the site of one of the wells, the other was stopped up in the eighteen-nineties; but the memory of the spa is preserved in the adjoining Wells Park.

The Hampstead of this southern group was Streatham—or perhaps Streatham people would reverse the order and say that Hampstead aspired to be to the north what Streatham was to the south. They might well have the better of the argument, for whereas Hampstead had a mere twenty years or so as a spa, Streatham had nearly three hundred years. Unlike most of the London springs, its waters were not affected by the laying of sewers and drains until the present century, when they suffered the inevitable fate and had to be cut off. The old London cry, 'Any fresh and fair spring water here?' is now a legend; but Streatham was the last of the old London spas to offer for sale any kind of medicinal water fresh from the earth. In character, Streatham Common has always been the typical spa green, and if it were farther away from the Capital the town would undoubtedly have remained as authentically a watering-place as Tunbridge Wells. The garrulous John Aubrey, rarest of gossips, was the first to describe it. In the *Natural History and Antiquities of Surrey* he tells us that the waters were discovered by field workers 'about fourteen years since,' which would be about 1659. He says: 'Afterwards at weeding time, the weeders being very dry, drinking of it, it purged them; by which accident its medicinal virtue was first discovered.' Not until 1671, however, was the water 'commonly drunk,' because up to that time the owner of the land forbade it. But Streatham's heyday was the eighteenth century, when the walks across the common were fashionable promenades and there were concerts at the wells every Monday and Thursday throughout the summer. Assemblies were held there until the middle of the century, if not later, in rooms which stood in the present Rookery Gardens. In 1757, Dr. Rutty, whose *Treatise on the Medicinal Waters of Great Britain and Ireland* was the most popular handbook to spa treatment in the middle of the eighteenth century, says of the Streatham wells: 'I found them situated on the declivity of a pleasant hill, about one hundred yards from the house on Streatham Green [Common]. I saw but two, the third had been filled up some time.' At this time Streatham waters were being sold in the London coffee-houses, where they were drunk to ward off attacks of the 'spleen' and other fashionable indispositions of the day.

The old well, which was closed in 1792, is now in the beautiful walled garden of The Rookery;[1] but shortly after the one was closed another, discovered about the end of the eighteenth century, came into use. It was this well that served The New Wells House, now painted white, which has a bust of Æsculapius over the front door and stands at the rear of the United Dairies premises in Valley Road.

But to bookmen, Streatham is the place where Dr. Johnson visited his friends the Thrales, who lived at Streatham Place and always kept a room ready to receive him. It is the place where he had his own chair at both table and hearth, the place he loved because there he could stretch his legs to the fire and have out his talk in peace. So dear did Streatham become to him that on bidding it farewell at his old friend's death he prayed that he might remember with gratitude the comforts and pleasures he had enjoyed there, and renounce them with holy submission, while for the two places of his special veneration, the kitchen and the church, his feelings were such that they could only be expressed in Latin.[2] Of this holy place little is left. Streatham Place has gone. But Sir Joshua Reynolds, another welcome guest at the Thrales' table, gave us a picture of the company that assembled there in the twenty-four portraits of the *Streatham Gallery*.

Richmond, the other fashionable spa south of the river, was yet one more discovery of the sixteen-eighties. Its well-house was opened in 1696, as we know from an advertisement in the *London Gazette* for April 20th to 23rd of that year, informing the public that 'The *New Wells* on Richmond Hill will be compleated for the reception of Company this following May. There is a large and lofty Dining Room, broad walks, open and shady, near 300 foot long, cut out of the descent of the Hill, with a prospect of all the country about.' Assembly-, card-, and raffling-rooms were added, where

[1] An account of The Rookery when in private hands appeared in *The Gardeners' Chronicle*, 20th November 1897.

[2] Boswell, vol. viii, p. 144.

lottery tickets could be bought to win anything from a gold chain to a well appointed equipage, where ombre and quadrille could be played, and where the most talked of beauties of the day could be met. It is interesting to notice that in most of the widely circulated advertisements for Richmond Spa particulars of the tides are given, suggesting that a considerable proportion of the patrons came by boat, though stables and coach-houses were certainly available. One of the wells, surmounted by a discarded ship's figurehead, remained in the garden of Cardigan House, Richmond Hill, until extensive alterations were made to the property soon after the British Legion acquired it in 1925-26. At that date, and for a number of years later, a tunnel, which at one time had been given the appearance of a grotto, passed beneath Petersham Road to connect the main part of the Cardigan House estate with a piece of land along the river bank. The riverside land was subsequently sold by the British Legion when the tow-path was widened.

Dr. John Evans, in *Richmond and its Vicinity*, says: 'Some of the oldest inhabitants of Richmond recollect there being a house and assembly-room adjoining the medicinal well.' Apparently, the character of the spa deteriorated during the last twenty-five years of its existence, particularly during the eighteen-fifties, when the price of admittance to the well was reduced, and in consequence a much rowdier company was attracted. Most of the residents were overjoyed, therefore, when the Misses Houblon, who founded the Houblon Almshouses in Marsh Gate Road, bought the property, and according to Mr. Richard Crisp, another Richmond historian, by 1870 the well-house had been pulled down and the gardens closed.

The last of London's country wells to flourish was Beulah, Upper Norwood, which belongs to the carriage-and-pair days of the early nineteenth century. Its pump-room, assembly-rooms, and hotel, were all designed by Decimus Burton, rebuilder of Tunbridge Wells, while its water was stated by Professor Faraday to be singularly strong in magnesium sulphate. Twenty-five acres of public gardens were laid out with all the adornments that the eighteen-thirties could devise, for it opened in August 1831 and closed in 1854. Its gardens are now divided among the villas that occupy their site. But before suburbia engulfed Beulah, coaches were run out daily from Charing Cross, and strings of Victorian parents conducted their numerous offspring to see the well, which was covered by a thatched hut shaped like an Indian wigwam, and, perhaps unwillingly, to drink its water before being allowed to marvel at the *camera obscura,* and to lose themselves in a maze whose involutions Dickens compared with those of Seven Dials. They would then picnic in a large booth thoughtfully provided

22 The Cold Baths, at Cold Bath Fields, London (1812)

23 'Dr. Lettsom, Fountain Cottage, Camberwell Grove, Surrey'
From a print by S. Rawle, 1803

24 The London and Bath Royal Patent Steam Coach

From an aquatint of c. 1820

for the purpose to avoid the disgrace of having litter strewn over the carefully tended gardens.

Mrs. Fitzherbert was a frequent visitor in the early days, and recommended the waters to her brother-in-law, the Duke of Gloucester, who came down to 'stimulate his jaded liver by potations at the spring.' A military band played daily from eleven till dusk the heartening tunes of Home and Empire, while bearded gentlemen in starched linen and well tailored suits reflected in their bearing the confidence of an age that had in prospect

> *Fifty years of ever-broadening Commerce!*
> *Fifty years of ever-brightening Science!*
> *Fifty years of ever-widening Empire!*

Chapter Five

BATH

'Twas a glorious sight to behold the fair sex
All wading with gentlemen, up to their necks,
And view them so prettily tumble and sprawl
In a big smoking kettle as big as our hall

The Bathes of Bathes Ayde

HITHERTO we have been occupied mainly with the vagaries of spa life. Here, terraced in the hills that slope down to the winding Avon, we see its greatest achievement, and that achievement one of the glories of the realm (2). Camps and earthworks of Celtic formation, and the legend of its foundation by Bladud, father of Shakespeare's King Lear, take us back to a time long before the Romans came and used its warm springs—the only springs in England to reach a temperature of 120° Fahrenheit. And to-day Bath still retains both socially and medicinally all that the other spas we have mentioned aspired to, or achieved, and, after enjoying for a few seasons, lost for ever. The origin of the hot springs at Bath is a subject for science, not social history. All we can say here is that we find in the neighbourhood the same exposure of strata found at other spas; but the hot water is said to well up through the New Red Sandstone and Lias from underlying palæozoic rocks. Other springs break through the oolitic formations on the slopes behind the city, but these are cold.

It is fitting, perhaps, that we should start by seeing the stone and water in this intimate relationship at Bath, because its fortunes have depended as much on the one as on the other. While Tunbridge Wells, Epsom, Hampstead, and the rest of them had their doctors, Bath alone among southern spas had architects who could express in worthy form the spirit of the cultured, leisured society that took its ease at the Georgian spas. The Woods, its builders, did more for the city than either the Olivers, its doctors, or the many royal persons who graced it with their patronage—Anne of Denmark, Catherine of Braganza, Queen Anne, or the early Georges.

Though its waters had been known so long, Bath as a social institution succeeded Tunbridge Wells, Epsom, and several other spas, and its character is affected by this later popularity. For all that, it is older as a resort than its architecture indicates. The Bath of the Woods, Beau Nash and the rest of them, rose from the ashes of an older, more casual and easy-going Bath. There could be no picknicking among the crescents of the new Bath as there had been in the fields of the old, or as there was on the furzy commons of Epsom or Tunbridge Wells. Once the Woods had imposed their Palladian magnificence on the old Somerset town, society was bound to become staid and matured—outwardly at all events. There could be no country-fair jollifications, as there had been earlier, and as there still were in Kent and Surrey. The Cavaliers had visited Bath; its society had sparkled with French vivacity; but under the Woods it became Augustan, and took its place in a different order. It was not necessarily a newer order. There was, in fact, more of the character of the Roman festival of Fontanalia in the new Bath than there was of that of the Belgian Spa, and it was appropriate that it should be so, because there are several remarkable remains of altars, a temple built in Corinthian style and dedicated to the goddess of healing, as well as the Roman baths themselves, which date from A.D. 54, but were hidden from the modern world until 1755, and not fully revealed until the excavations, begun in 1877 and still in progress, were well advanced. They leave us in no doubt about the importance of their *Aquae Sulis* to the Romans. The Great Bath is 73 feet by 29½ feet, surrounded by dressing-rooms and steps under a gallery supported by pillars.

Sul, the Celtic goddess of springs, identified by the Romans with their own Minerva, protected the bathers, and for three hundred and fifty years her votaries brought their offerings and implored her favours. Legionaries from the North were brought here to recuperate; invalids from the Continent came over to bathe in the waters; the fame of the Somerset town extended until in the third century Solinus, a Latin grammarian, described it as one of the wonders of the world. 'In Britain,' he writes, 'are hot springs furnished luxuriously for human use. Over these springs Minerva presides, and in her temple the perpetual fire never whitens into ash, but as the flame fades, turns into rocky balls.'

When the legions left Britain in A.D. 410 the baths were deserted and the city lost its culture. Its history during the next six hundred years is obscure. In Domesday, Bath appears as a royal borough, and two years later it became the headquarters of a see, transferred for greater convenience from Wells until by a famous compromise the two sees were combined in the middle of the twelfth century. The new bishop, John of Tours, raised a noble cathedral on the site of the old monastic church, then in ruins, and by his zeal gave Bath the ecclesiastical character it still retains, with the sixteenth-century abbey, though much smaller than the cathedral of Bishop John, dominating the plan. Meanwhile the townsfolk earned their livelihood spinning and weaving, as we are reminded by Chaucer's Wife of Bath, of whom we read that,

> *Of clooth-making she hadde swiche an haunt,*
> *She passed hem of Ypres and of Gaunt.*

Of the springs we hear little until Leland discovered them in the fifteen-thirties. 'Or ever I came to the bridge of Bath,' he writes, 'that is over the Avon I came down a rocky hill full of fair springs of water; and on this rocky hill is set a long street as a suburb to the city of Bath; and by this street is a chapel of St. Mary Magdalen. There is a great gate with a stone arch at the entry of the bridge.' He goes on to describe the city walls and many curious carvings remaining as 'testimony of the antiquity of the town.' He tells us that the Cross Bath, so called because it had a cross in the centre, was frequented by people suffering from leprosy, pock, scabs, and various aches and pains. The Hot Bath, also, he describes, and the King's Bath, which was much in favour with the gentlemen of the city.

More than a generation later—in 1577—Harrison of Radwinter, an Essex parson, described the scene in his *Description of England*. Bath, he says, was then resorted to by the nobility, the gentry, the commonalty and the clergy, and, somewhat surprisingly, he commends the place for its cleanliness, which was not a prominent characteristic to the minds of most observers. Of the Bath of Leland and Harrison little is left except a few fragments behind Broad Street, in Westgate Street, a number of interior features, notably in the Christopher Hotel and the Sedan Chair Café, and, of course, Sally Lunn's house in Lilliput Alley.

If we start on the city's record of distinguished visitors we shall run through twenty or thirty pages without pausing for breath; but so much of the glory that was Bath lives on in letters, diaries, novels, and reminiscences that we must have at least a selection of what has been said about it. Besides the exalted, the obscure travelled for days in great discomfort to take advantage of the waters. Almost every parish must have records such as these from Danbury in Essex, where, in 1640, twenty-five shillings was given 'to Medcalfe to go to The Bath,' and in 1728 William Ffytche, the squire, is recorded as being buried 'from Ye Bath,' where, apparently, he had died.[1] After spending the night at a wayside inn on Salisbury Plain, where the beds were good but lousy, and for that reason made the party merry, Pepys visited Bath for the first time on the 12th June 1668. Mrs.

[1] *Danbury*, Mary Hopkirk.

Pepys was a native of Somerset, so she was 'mightily pleased' to be home, especially as Samuel was so genially disposed as to commend the county. The baths he found 'not so large' as he had imagined them, 'but yet pleasant; and the town most of stone, and clean, though the streets generally narrow.' But of the Cross Bath, which he visited next day in the company of his wife, Betty Turner, Willet, and W. Hewer, he says that he saw there 'very fine ladies; and the manner pretty enough, only methinks it cannot be clean to go so many bodies together in the same water.' That is rather different from what William Harrison said; but of course the Cross Bath was now ninety years

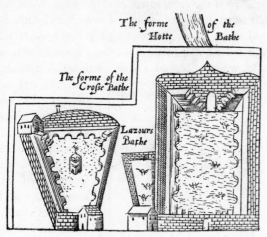

The forme
Hotte
of the
Bathe

The forme of the
Crosse Bathe

Lazours
Bathe

25 *From a map of* 1610

older. Nineteen years later again the cross that Pepys saw was replaced by the beautiful, though curiously un-English, 'Modena' Cross erected to celebrate the visit of James II's Italian consort in 1687. Artistically it must have been a fine piece of work; but its symbolism was offensive to a Protestant nation, and in the forties of the following century it was destroyed by an anti-Jacobite mob. After the first attack it was repaired; but the fervour of the '45 was too much for it. An inoffensive urn and crown took its place, with little more than the actual cross surviving from the 'Modena' composition.

Mary of Modena was yet one more English queen who visited the baths in the hope of finding in their waters strength to bring an heir to the throne. The city already had its Queen's Bath as well as its King's Bath. The latter is now by far the most important memorial of seventeenth-century Bath. The Cross Bath is altered past recognition, and much of the Queen's Bath we see to-day is Victorian; but it has Jacobean survivals to remind us that it was here that Anne of Denmark, queen of James I, bathed in 1616. From her this second of the baths still in use, built by a Mr. Bellot in 1597, took its name. It was important that the 1616 visit should have a permanent memorial, because this was the royal visit that again made bathing fashionable. After the queen's visit the Somerset country folk crowded into the city in such numbers that John Wood said 'The baths were like so many bear gardens, and modesty was entirely shut out of them; people of both sexes bathing by day and night naked.' Forty-seven years later society again flocked to Bath after the visit of Catherine of Braganza, who, when the cold waters of Tunbridge Wells proved ineffective, came west to try the warm springs of Bristol and Bath. But important as these royal visits were, Bath was still a very humble ancestor of the city that inherited its long traditions. Celia Fiennes, who was there in or before 1687, wrote: 'The ways to the Bath are all difficult, the town lies low in

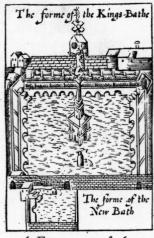

The forme of the Kings-Bathe

The forme of the New Bath

26 *From a map of* 1610

a bottom and its steep ascents all ways out of the town; the houses are indifferent, the streets of a good size well pitched . . . the baths in my opinion make the town unpleasant, the air thick and hot by their steam, and by its own situation so low, encompassed with high hills and woods.'

When Celia Fiennes was at Bath the ladies stepped into the water in special gowns 'made of a fine yellow canvas, which is stiff and made large with great sleeves like a parson's gown.' This, she says, concealed the figure effectively; but it must have been an extremely uncomfortable garment. In leaving, the bather passed through a wooden door while still in the water, and thus gained privacy for ascending the steps leading to a dressing-room, where an attendant was ready with warm slippers and a flannel garment shaped like a nightgown. These dressing rooms were called slips. They were fitted with fireplaces, and care was taken that the bather should not be in danger of catching a chill. By the end of the century ladies of fashion could bathe with perfect decorum. They would bring with them, or hire at the bath, specially made japanned bowls, which on entering the water they would tie to their arms with ribbons. These would serve all the purposes of the modern lady's handbag—except, of course, to conceal secrets! Handkerchief, nosegay, perfumes and smelling salts, and, in the eighteenth century, snuff box and patches, would all be trailed along in this tiny boat, while the bathers spent an hour in light-hearted conversation, exchanging jests and compliments, or listening to the music played for their entertainment. Afterwards they would be carried home in sedan-chairs, and after dressing would assemble again at the pump-room.

The rest of the day followed much the same course as that already traced at Tunbridge. There was a service—we cannot say prayers—at the abbey. The scene is well described in *A Step to the Bath* (1700): "'tis crowded during Divine Service as much as St. Paul's, in which time there is more Billet Deaux [sic] convey'd to the Ladies than Notes to desire the Prayers of the Congregation at B.'s Meeting-House, and as the Ingenious Doctor in his Discourse told the Audience: He was afraid most of them came more out of Custome and Formality than in Devotion to the Sacred Deity, or a suitable Reverence to the Place of Worship, which was very True I am confident, and the Ladies were the only Saints several came there to Adore.' In the same work there is an animated description of the evening resort, the bowling green: 'About five in the Evening we went to see a great match of Bowling; there was Quality, and Reverend Doctors of both Professions, Topping Merchants, Broken Bankers, Noted Mercers, Inns of Court Rakes, City Beaux, Stray'd Prentices and Dancing-Masters in abundance. *Fly, fly, fly, fly,* said one; *Rub, rub, rub, rub,* cry'd another. *Ten guineas to Five I uncover the Jack,* says a Third. *Damn these nice Fingers of mine,* cry'd my Lord, *I Slipt my Bowl and mistook the Bias.* Another swearing he knew the ground to an inch, and would hold Five Pounds his Bowl came in. But in short, the Citizens won the Courtiers' money, and the Courtiers swore to be reveng'd on their Wives and Daughters.' Most of the day's amusements were still in the open air. Dancing, for example, was outdoors more often than indoors. Indeed, at the Restoration and for many years afterwards there was no indoor dancing at the spas. Tunbridge Wells had no ball-room when Catherine of Braganza and her ladies were there. They danced on the bowling green. Indoor dancing was unknown at the spas until the end of the seventeenth century. It is said to have been introduced by the Duke of Beaufort, whose seat, Badminton, was fourteen miles from Bath. According to the story he started the custom of dancing indoors by leading the company from the green to the Town Hall on a memorable occasion.

As may be guessed, all that has been said about the dissolute life of worthless hangers-on of the Caroline courts in Tunbridge Wells and Epsom can be assumed of the society at Bath. If possible, as we shall see in the next chapter, Bath exceeded its rivals in licentiousness and folly. Its remoteness from London made it safer from the prying eyes of London gossips, though it had plenty of its own. Indeed, from the visit of Charles II in 1663 until Bath got a king of its own in Beau Nash this was the Devil's own playground, particularly when the centre of attraction shifted from the baths to the gaming tables, because it was gambling, not bathing that brought wealth to the southern spas.

The order imposed on this chaos by Richard Nash (28), himself a gambler and by no means immune from original sin, is a remarkable example of what can be done by the force of sheer personality. This astonishing creature was born at Swansea in 1674. He was educated at Carmarthen Grammar School and Jesus College, Oxford, from which he was sent down for a youthful indiscretion before reaching the age of seventeen. His biographer, Oliver Goldsmith, says 'in college he soon showed that though much might be expected from his genius, nothing could be hoped from his industry.' After failing to distinguish himself as a scholar, he tried his fortune as a soldier and lawyer, and when he walked into Bath along with several companions in 1705 his only object was to try his luck at the gaming tables. In that apparently inauspicious way began a triumphant career that lasted more than fifty-five years, and ended with an abbey funeral that would have done honour to a royal duke.

The turn in Nash's favour came soon after his arrival, with the death of the city's Master of Ceremonies, a man named Webster, who was killed in a duel. Nash applied for the post, and though his only claim to qualification was that he had made a considerable success of a small venture as Master of the Revels in the Middle Temple, he was appointed. With great daring he immediately assumed the role of Absolute Monarch, and carried himself with such an air that few, apparently, ever had the temerity to question his authority. To have maintained so exalted a position so long, and in so curiously assorted a society, Nash must obviously have been a man of quite exceptional range of character and enterprise. His skill in handling both men and women of every rank, condition, and degree can seldom have been surpassed. Under his rule, balls that had hitherto been noisy revels became orderly and dignified events. Each began with the gentleman of the highest rank present leading out the lady of the highest rank for a minuet. At the end the lady was led back to her seat and the beau brought forward a second partner for the gentleman. After the second dance both retired, to be followed by every couple in the room in precisely the same manner, each gentleman dancing with two ladies, and all selected by Nash himself. This solemn, and one would think tedious, minuet might occupy as much as two hours. Then came free-and-easy country dances until nine, when refreshments were served, and these might be quite a banquet. 'In my last,' wrote Sarah Robinson to her sister, Mrs. Montagu, the blue-stocking, in 1745, 'I mentioned I was going to the ball; there was a table of sweetmeats, jellies, wine, biscuits, cold ham and turkey set behind two screens, which

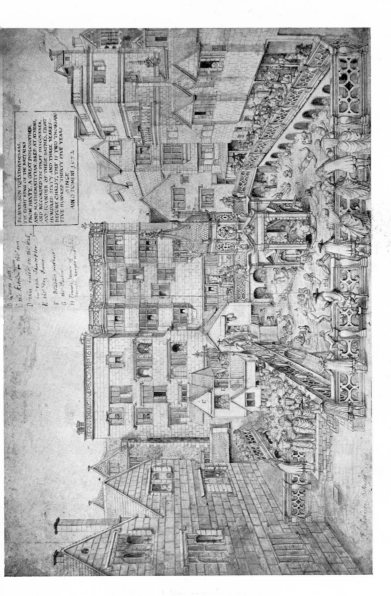

27 Bath. The King's Bath (*right*) and Queen's Bath (*left*) in 1672

From a contemporary drawing by Thomas Johnson

28 Beau Nash, 1674–1762

By an unknown artist

at nine o'clock were taken away, and the table discovered . . . Above stairs there was a hot supper, for all that would take the trouble to go up.'

On the stroke of eleven Nash stepped forward and held up his hand as a signal for the musicians to stop playing. They stopped on the instant. Even when the Princess Amelia, whom we met at Islington, called for one dance more the Beau replied graciously, but with a firmness that left the princess abashed, that the laws of Bath were as unalterable as those of Lycurgus, the Spartan. About dress he was equally strict. On one occasion the Duchess of Queensberry appeared in an apron of point lace, said to be of great value. Nash disapproved, and immediately requested her grace to remove it. She complied without question. He alone was allowed an elaborate, original costume, of which the most notable feature was the famous white hat. At a ball given in 1734 in honour of the king's birthday he appeared in gold lace so resplendent that Lord Chesterfield, who was present, declared that at a distance he looked for all the world like a gilt garland.

Though Nash was a sleeping-partner in one of the gambling houses at Bath, and gambling was obviously the source of his personal fortune, he was always ready to warn off the tables those who could not afford to take risks. There is the story of the young earl he took in hand. Seeing that unless this young gallant learnt his lesson quickly he would be penniless, Nash himself engaged him in play and steadily won from him his entire fortune, including the title deeds of his estates, and finally even the watch in his pocket and rings on his fingers. Then he frightened the life out of the young man by making his position plain to him. Finally, with a magnificent gesture, on receiving from the youth a promise never to play for money again, the Beau threw on the table everything he had won and sent the earl about his business. It is a revealing story; but perhaps we get the keenest insight into Nash's character in the tale of his encounter with Sarah Duchess of Marlborough. Nash was one of the founders and principal supporters of the Bath Hospital. One day when he was trying to raise funds for it the duchess seemed bent on avoiding him. But there was no way of eluding Richard Nash. At last he found her and asked for a subscription. The duchess smiled graciously and said:

'You must put down a trifle for me, Nash, for I have no money in my pockets.'

'Yes, Madam, that I will do with pleasure, if your Grace will tell me when to stop,' he replied; and taking a handful of guineas from his pocket he threw them one by one into his hat.

'One, Two, Three, Four, Five.'

'Hold! Hold!' cried the duchess, 'consider what you are about.'

'Madam, consider your rank and fortune,' retorted Nash; 'Six, Seven, Eight, Nine, Ten.' The guineas dropped merrily in spite of the duchess's protests.

'Pray compose yourself, Madam,' said the Beau, 'do not interfere with the work of charity . . . Eleven, Twelve, Thirteen, Fourteen, Fifteen.'

Again the duchess pleaded for mercy; but the Beau's lips were firmly set, though doubtless there was a twinkle in his eye.

'You shall have your name written in letters of gold, and upon the front of the building, too,' he promised as he counted 'Seventeen, Eighteen, Nineteen, Twenty.'

'Hold!' cried the duchess imperiously, 'I will not pay a farthing more.'

'Charity covers a multitude of sins,' remarked Nash, still unperturbed: 'Twenty-one, Twenty-two, Twenty-three, Twenty-four, Twenty-five.'

'Nash, I protest, you frighten me out of my wits. Lord! I shall die.'

'Madam, you will never die doing good,' he laughed, 'and even if you did, it would be the better for you.'

He was about to plunge his hand into his pocket for more guineas, but the duchess became serious and Nash saw that he had gone as far as he could, so they settled for thirty guineas.

It was under Nash's rule that Bath became the foremost spa in England, though undoubtedly circumstances were peculiarly in his favour. Three years before he arrived, Queen Anne and her consort had paid a visit, and on that occasion a hundred young men of Bath and two hundred women and girls had ridden out to the county boundary to meet the royal party and escort them to the city. So many visitors had flocked into Bath in the queen's wake that as much as a guinea a night had been paid for a bed, and no doubt was still being paid when Nash took up his appointment as Master of Ceremonies.

Here, then, was a state of affairs that called for talents beyond the compass of any one man, even of a Richard Nash. A new city must be built to cater for the visitors who came in ever increasing numbers. There were eight thousand in 1715, and the Saracen's Head in Broad Street, dated 1713, two or three other inns and a few lodging houses, were quite inadequate to provide for their needs. But as Bath got its Beau at the right moment, it also got its builder. After ten years of increasing prosperity under Nash, that is to say in 1715, a young Cornishman named Ralph Allen crossed the bridge and entered the city to take up an appointment as clerk in the post office. As with Nash, there was nothing in the circumstances of his arrival to foreshadow the importance of the event for Bath. But again the man was of exceptional talent and exceptional strength of character. He was sufficiently diligent in his own profession to become postmaster, and sufficiently enterprising to organise a system of cross-posts between England and Wales that entitles him to be considered one of the founders of our modern postal service. But these undertakings only absorbed a small part of his immense energy. He invented means of conveying the stone from the Combe Down quarries, which he bought, to a point from which it could be carried by water to Bristol and London. And what is more to our point, he conceived the idea of building a new Bath from this stone, a Bath that would be supported by visitors who came to take the waters, and eventually by residents also. But for so great an enterprise as this he needed capital and an architect.

It is, perhaps, worth remarking at this stage that the elegance and stateliness of the Bath we see to-day had no sort of connection with any art-for-art's-sake nonsense. It was a commercial undertaking in the first place. Allen saw that there was gold in these waters, and he determined to have some of it in his own pockets. In order to gain enough capital to start the enterprise he married the illegitimate daughter of General Wade, bachelor Member of Parliament for Bath, who is said to have been indebted to him for a political service. His architect he found in Yorkshire in John Wood, a man as hard-headed and practical as himself. Between them they planned a town that would draw and hold wealthy and aristocratic visitors, the kind of visitors who would leave money behind them. No doubt the commercial instinct was stronger in Allen than it was in Wood. Palladian architecture was then the rage. Wood was obviously an enthusiast for it, and when he learned that the original Bath had been created by Rome he was evidently fired by a desire to raise up from its ruins, as it were, a second Rome. The idea, no doubt, appealed to Allen because he saw at once that this Palladian magnificence would both flatter rank and entice riches. So Corinthian columns and Roman pediments were much to the taste of these two ambitious men. The result was the city we still see. To the mathematician it must be Paradise, even though to other orders of men its appeal may vary according to their taste or distaste for the formal. It was particularly fortunate that Wood had been a surveyor, because this meant that lay-out as well as construction was always in the front of his mind. He thought naturally in terms of circuses, terraces, and crescents, as well as in terms of facades and elevations, and though he did not live to see his work completed he was succeeded by a son whose main object in life was to finish what his father had begun. Queen Square, begun in 1728-9 and finished seven years later, was the father's masterpiece. The Circus, a more spectacular achievement, was planned by the father and executed by the son. The Royal Crescent, the culmination of the work of these two remarkable men, was the son's work, but so harmonious with the father's that the two must always be thought of together. One of the most delightful things about the elder Wood's achievement is that it was an amateur's. He was never trained as an architect. In this, if in little else, Bath was a typically English product, for in no other European country does the amateur triumph so often as in England.

To see and to be seen had always been an important element in spa life, parades of some kind were therefore necessities. Before the Woods these had been improvised rather than designed. At Bath they were conceived on the grand scale afterwards adopted for all resorts, whether inland or coastal, and it is worth noting that the promenades of our seaside watering-places have common ancestors in the parades of Bath and the Pantiles of Tunbridge Wells.

It could hardly be expected that so ambitious a man as Ralph Allen would see so many fine houses going up in Bath, and hear such accounts as Wood could give him of the houses that he and his rival, Colin Campbell, were building for the rich in other parts of the kingdom, without desiring a mansion of his own that would, if possible, outshine the rest. So the magnificence of Prior Park is not to be wondered at. It is obvious that in designing it Wood was trying to outshine Colin Campbell's achievement, Wanstead House, built for Earl Tylney in Epping Forest.

Ralph Allen was a self-made, purse-proud man, and if there were no other sides to his character than those already suggested we might find him remarkable, but neither attractive nor admirable. But he had, in fact, elements of greatness that inspired both respect and affection, and Prior Park was to be more than its owner's show-piece. By the warmth of Allen's hospitality, and by his discernment in selecting guests, it became one of the great country houses of the eighteenth century, and one with a permanent place in literary history. Post-master Allen was the respected friend of Pope, who wrote of him in the Epilogue to his *Satires* (Dial. i. 135-6):

> *Let humble Allen, with an awkward shame,*
> *Do good by stealth, and blush to find it fame.*

Fielding enjoyed his hospitality and repaid it by making a combination of Allen and Lord Lyttelton the Squire Allworthy of his *Tom Jones*. Gainsborough, Garrick, and Quin were guests at Prior Park, and Pitt, the Great Commoner, who had a house in Bath, frequently sat at Allen's table. Pitt was Member of Parliament for Bath from 1757 to 1766, and on Allen's death wrote to the widow: 'I will only say that, in Mr. Allen, mankind has lost such a benevolent and tender friend as, I fear, not all the example of his virtues will have power to raise up to the world again. Admiring his life and regretting the shortness of it, I shall ever respectfully cherish his memory, and rank the continuation of the favourable opinion and friendship of a truly good man amongst the happiest advantages and the first honours which fortune may have bestowed on my life.'

Between them, Allen and the Woods raised up a city designed to be something more than the playgrounds for fashion and gallantry that Epsom, Tunbridge Wells, the London spas, and Bath itself had been. In Bath, culture and taste found a home such as they had not hitherto had in England. There are admirable guides to the architecture of the city, notably Mr. Bryan Little's. Here we are concerned with its social achievement, which amounts to this: in Bath the youthful brilliance of Epsom and Tunbridge Wells matured into the elegance and charm of the most accomplished social life England has ever known outside the capital. Landor described Bath as the English Florence. It was hardly that, but the comparison is interesting because it again emphasises that there was more of the Italian than of the French about it. The Restoration court, which first introduced into England the fashionable life on which the spas were to flourish, had been superseded by a large new class of more responsible noblemen, country gentlemen, and well-to-do merchants. The second class were particularly important. The Revolution of 1688 had established the landed gentry, and the recent increase in public wealth had given them a taste for polite society. Bath thus became the new school of manners. The nobility patronised it, and the gentry followed because in Bath, better than anywhere else, they could study the ways of those they wished to emulate. Hitherto fashionable life had been restricted to the court, now it had penetrated to another stratum of society, and it is amusing to trace through the letters and journals of the period the snobbery and uncertainty of the newly exalted. Pepys is an admirable example. As always with the newly initiated, fear of making mistakes was universal. That is why the strict rules of Beau Nash were such a comfort. The old and small aristocracy had been able to indulge in the wildest pranks unquestioned. The new rich must keep to the book of rules, and everything about Bath helped them. At the same time the architecture gave them all the sense of importance their ambitious hearts could desire. In a sense, society had come full circle. Henrietta Maria and her ladies had lived in tents on the common at Tunbridge Wells and loved it. Theirs had been an escape from magnificence into freedom. The new society at Bath sought instead to escape from a freedom it was not capable of using into a magnificence where everything was arranged for it on the grandest scale, and in which all the people had to do was pay. They bought, as it were, tickets for social security.

In the early days the scene must have been farcical. Only in a chaos of uncertainty could such men as Nash and Allen, enterprising and determined as they were, have gained so speedy and decisive an ascendancy. They gave the people what they needed—rule and order. Let psychologists and moralists work out the reasons, the fact is that the new leisured class found relief from the burden of the social insecurity they had previously borne, in the ceremony, the decorum, and the formality of the new Bath. The wildest folly was carried through with the solemnity of an abbey service, which made nonsense of the abbey service but somehow helped with the folly.

Immediately they entered the city each family or party came under the rule of the Master of Ceremonies. A peal of the abbey bells announced the arrival, followed by a visit of the city waits to the favoured inn or lodging house. The Master of Ceremonies then called to pay his respects, and before many hours had passed subscriptions would have been collected for pump- and assembly-rooms, promenades, circulating libraries and every other local institution, for there was no such thing as private pleasure or any form of anonymity for visitors to eighteenth-century spas. What a scene it was for the novelist and play-wright! And how excellently Smollett, Sheridan, Jane Austen, Fanny Burney, and, in the nineteenth century, Dickens and Thackeray made use of it!

Of the place of Bath in literature Macauley said: 'The genius of Anstey and Smollett, Frances Burney and Miss Austen, made it classic ground.' Pope was fascinated by the comedy of manners he saw before him whichever way he turned. The parades he thought the finest in the world; the company delighted him. Writing to Theresa and Martha Blount in October 1714 he said: 'I have slid, I can't tell how, into all the amusements of the place. My whole day is shared by the Pump assemblies, the walks, the chocolate-houses, raffling-shops, medleys &c . . . I endeavour (like all awkward fellows) to become agreeable by imitation: and, observing who are most in favour with the fair, I sometimes copy the civil air of Gascoin, sometimes the impudent one of Nash, and sometimes for vanity, the silly one of a neigh-bour of yours, who has lost to the gamesters here that money of which the ladies only deserve to rob a man of his age.' Hardly a luminary of the age—literary, political, clerical, or learned—failed to present himself at the pump-room at least once, and the amusements enlivened even such grave divines as Bishops Butler and Berkeley, such pious ladies as Selina, Countess of Huntingdon and Hannah More, who in January 1792 wrote: 'Bath, happy Bath, is as gay as if there were no war, nor sin, nor misery in the world! . . . Yet it is the fashion to affect to be religious, and to show it by inveighing against the wickedness of France! I really know many who believe they are pious on no other ground.' Porson came, and scandalised the elegant citizens by appearing in the assembly-rooms with uncombed hair, carelessly tied neckcloth and wrinkled stockings.

But it is not the wrinkled stockings of Porson, it is the blue-stockings of the literary ladies that we are so amused to remember in Bath. And in truth it is the ladies, with their eyes for detail, their sparkle, and their occasional malice, who have left us the best descriptions of spa life. In *Evelina*, Fanny Burney says: 'The charming city of Bath answered all my expectations. The Crescent, the prospect from it, and the elegant symmetry of the Circus, delighted me. The Parades, I own, rather disappointed me; one of them is scarce preferable to some of the best paved streets in London; and the other, though it affords a beautiful prospect, a charming view of Prior-park and of the Avon, yet wanted something in *itself* of more striking elegance than a mere broad pavement, to satisfy the ideas I had formed of it.

'At the pump-room, I was amazed at the public exhibition of the ladies in the bath; it is true, their heads are covered with bonnets; but the very idea of being seen, in such a situation by whoever pleases to look, is indelicate.'

Miss Burney stayed at Bath with the Thrales in 1780. They occupied a house at the riverside corner of South Parade, and Fanny's room would have the view she described. While there she seems to have made the acquaintance of everyone in the city worth knowing, particularly Lady Miller of Bath Easton, the Lady of the Vase. Lady Miller and her husband turned their house into the local Temple of the Muses. They had literary parties every Thursday evening, at which prizes were given for verses on prescribed topics. When written, the verses were dropped into an enormous Roman vase decked with myrtle and pink ribbon. The following week they were taken out and judged; whereupon the winner was presented to the Lady of the Vase, and allowed to kneel before her and kiss her hand. Finally, she set a crown of myrtle upon the august poetic brows.

Dr. Johnson had a poor opinion of Lady Miller, whose parties Miss Burney thought so 'tonish.' He said bluntly that any man who dropped verses into the vase 'was a blockhead for his pains.' The doctor, it may be recalled, was at Bath with the Thrales in 1776. By this time Nash had been dead fifteen years and Johnson was the lion of the season, which was one of the most brilliant in the city's history. Sheridan's *Rivals* was being played to packed houses, while at the Octagon, the beautiful Miss Linley, with whom Sheridan subsequently eloped, was holding large audiences spell-bound with her voice, or person, or both. The excesses of the earlier Bath had passed, and by now as likely as not a bishop instead of a playboy would be found at the centre of a laughing circle of admiring auditors. The Bishop of Peterborough, it may be remembered, preached one morning in the abbey at the express wish of Mrs. Thrale, and afterwards proposed a 'frolic,' which on this occasion meant an outing to Spring Gardens, where the bishop promised to entertain everybody to tea. The bishop's treat turned out to be a raree-show at the home of an alderman of the city, a Mr. Ferry, whose house was full of booby-traps and mechanical contrivances of the Heath-Robinson type. For example, a trap-door opened to allow a table to spring up from the floor, while a similar door in the ceiling opened to let down an eagle with extended claws, which caught up and flew off with a cloth thrown over the table, leaving the delighted guests to enjoy a glorious spread of sweetmeats, cakes, and jellies. In *Humphry Clinker* (1771), Jerry Melford observed: 'There is always a great show of the clergy at Bath; none of your thin, puny, yellow, hectic figures, exhausted with abstinence and hard study, labouring under the *morbi eruditorium*; but great overgrown dignitaries and rectors, with rubicund noses and gouty ancles, or broad bloated faces, dragging along great swag bellies; the emblems of sloth and indigestion.' Such did Bath become in the last decades of the eighteenth century.

But the worst was still to be. In *Northanger Abbey,* of which nineteen of the thirty chapters are set in Bath, and *Persuasion,* with nine chapters in Bath, we see how the high spirits of the Bath of Beau Nash and Ralph Allen had given place to exclusiveness and snobbery. Jane Austen had visited the city two or three times earlier, but her real knowledge of Bath life dates from 1800, when she went to live at 4, Sydney Place, with her father, the Rev. George Austen, who that year retired from his living at Steventon in Hampshire. It was not a happy move for Jane; but a most favourable one for letters. And still the process of decay continued. If the Bath of Jane Austen had lost its youthful vigour, that of Dickens was old and tired. Its stuffiness is felt in almost every line of the part of *Pickwick Papers* describing life at Bath, with the Dowager Lady Snuphanuph, the rich Lord Mutanhed, and the Honourable Mr. Crushton exchanging inane compliments with each other and with Angelo Cyrus Bantam Esq., Grand Master of Ceremonies. By this time the young sparks of society were disporting themselves at Brighton and Scarborough. As R. A. L. Smith says in his book on *Bath*: 'A symbol of the change in Bath society from the ultra-fashionable to the ultra-respectable is the substitution of the bath-chair for the sedan-chair as the mode of conveyance for invalids.... By the accession of Queen Victoria, 1837, the sedan-chairs had all disappeared from the streets, squares, and crescents of Bath. The bath-chairs, dull, monotonous, respectable, were to be seen everywhere in all their cold and drab unloveliness.'

29 The Portico and Entrance
From an aquatint by J. C. Nattes, 1806

30 The Colonnades
From an engraving after Spornberg, c. 1795

BATH: THE PUMP ROOM

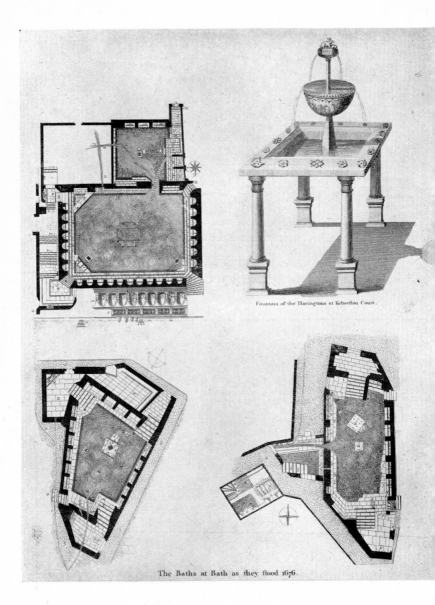

Fountain of the Haringtons at Kelwefton Court.

The Baths at Bath as they ftood 1676.

31 BATH. An eighteenth-century print showing the various baths as they were in 1676. The King's Bath is at *top left*, the Queen's Bath at *bottom right*

For all that, there was much to be said for the bath-chair. It brought money to Bath. With the decline of the spa as a pleasure resort came its rise as a place of residence for elderly, well-to-do gentlefolk of the commodious twenty-shillings-in-the-pound era.

Then, in the second half of the nineteenth century, came the revival of the spa, and the progressive introduction of scientific treatment until to-day Bath claims to have unsurpassed hydrological and electrical equipment for use with the hot springs, which give out half a million gallons of the most highly radio-active mineral water in the kingdom. Bath might well be thought to have passed from a romantic to a purely utilitarian function. But this city with two thousand years of recorded history is more than a place of healing, great as that is, and more than the noble monument we see as we look down on its grey stone houses from the encircling hills, or up to them from one of its fine bridges. It is still a city with a secret, and therefore a place to fascinate the minds of all the more enquiring orders of men. Archaeologists have worked on it and published their findings, and at the time I write—April 1950—a young Bristol geologist is causing a stir by claiming to have discovered a deposit of more than a hundred thousand tons of uranium bearing ore in the hills between Bath and Bristol. Few responsible scientists are prepared at the moment to venture an opinion on the worth of this claim. It has long been known that the waters of Bath must have some uranium content in them, but whether the deposit would justify lifting or not is more than anyone can calculate at present. So the secret of the springs is still hidden, and Bath retains its lure as well as its legends.

32 Queen Charlotte in the Pump Room, 1817

Chapter Six

LES EAUX DE SCANDALE

Light-fingered knaves, who pockets drill,
Wits, captains, politicians, trulls,
Sots, devotees, pimps, poets, gulls.
THE HUMOURS OF TUNBRIDGE WELLS

THERE was a time, we are told, when a pure water was as rare as a pure woman—and when the two were considered equally insipid. Neither, it seems, was to be expected at the Caroline and Georgian spas. The medicinal value of the one was in its impurity; and so, we must believe, was the social value of the other. 'They should be called the Waters of Scandal,' said the Duc de Cominges, French ambassador, in 1663, referring to Tunbridge Wells, 'for they have gone nigh to ruining all the women and girls of reputation (I mean such as had not their husbands with them).' The particular scandal the ambassador had in mind arose from the much discussed purpose of the queen's visit. She had come, as we have seen, to drink the waters in the vain hope that they would enable her to bear a child. With Tunbridge, then, the scandal actually came from the company, not from the waters. Indeed it was slyly suggested that the gallants, not the wells, cured the visiting ladies of barrenness:

From these the Waters got the Reputation
Of good assistants unto Generation.

In the Prologue to *Tunbridge Walks* we have the lines:

Where Beaux, and City Wives in Medley come,
The brisk Gallant supplies the Husband's room,
While he, dear, harmless Cuckold, packs up Goods at home.

The king, or course, was no 'harmless Cuckold.' With Charles and Catherine it was not the wife's but the husband's love affairs that caused the trouble. We first hear in detail about the scandalous conduct of this licentious court from Count Anthony Hamilton, who in the *Memoirs of the Count de Gramont* describes its tangle of intrigues and amours. After dealing

74

with plans for the proposed visit of the Court to Tunbridge, he adds tersely: 'Miss Stewart, more handsome than ever, was appointed for this excursion, and began to make magnificent preparations. The poor queen durst say nothing against it, but all hopes of success immediately forsook her.' In other words, the waters could never cure the queen's sterility while the king's affections were engaged elsewhere.

Under such circumstances as these, what more likely than that the wags of Tunbridge, eyeing the queen and her ladies in the lewd bold manner of the age should snigger and whisper that they saw no sign of pregnancy in the queen, but, with a ribald oath, that every other lady of the Court looked like being brought to bed with a sturdy boy. And indeed there may have been more substance in the jest than we think. Life in the tents set up on the common was notoriously unrestrained. There had been a long war, aggravated by all the repressions of Puritan rule, and now that the king was on his throne again—and the merriest king since the eighth Harry—it was only to be expected that mirth should gain on morals. 'Never,' says the count, 'did Love behold his Empire so flourishing as here. Those who had been smitten before coming felt their ardour redoubled, and those who seemed the least susceptible of love lost all their austerity, and became different beings.' But the count himself was by no means scandalised. He was a member of the naughty circle and found the life delicious. It was the Puritan clergy—and they were strong in Tunbridge— who brought out the immorality, and if we were inclined that way, no doubt we could learn more of the prurient elements in Caroline society from such sermons as *A Discourse against the fashion of spots, naked breasts and powder for the hair*, by F. Hawkins (1664), or *A just and seasonable Reprehension of the enormity of naked breasts and shoulders, written by a grave and learned Papist*— in actual fact a Puritan—than from any court reminiscences. These were the ancestors of the type described in forthright Yorkshire style by Mrs. Dean in *Wuthering Heights*, of one of whom she said: 'He was, and is yet most likely, the wearisomest, self-righteous Pharisee that ever ransacked a Bible to rake the promises to himself, and fling the curses on his neighbours.'

It was undoubtedly the Londoners who took the scandalous elements into the country, and did so from the days when Epsom and Tunbridge Wells first flourished, to the Regency, when the spas sowed their last wild oats. In Shadwell's play *Epsom Wells* we read: 'But if you were not so monstrous lewd, the freedom of Epsom allows almost nothing to be scandalous.' And in 1713 we find Steele, in discussing the scandal-mongering of jealous-minded people in the *Guardian* No. 174, saying that this is worst in the

spas. 'I have had reams of letters,' he tells us, 'from Bath, Epsom, Tunbridge, and St. Wenefrede's Well.' There were so many of them, he says,
that he determined to visit Bath, for he was told 'that more constitutions
were weakened there than repaired; that the physicians were not more busy
in destroying old bodies, than the young fellows were in producing new
ones; with several other common-place strokes at raillery.' So he bought
himself an embroidered cap and brocade night-gown and went down to
Somerset to see the spa for himself.

The belief that spa water promoted fertility dates from the Roman
festival of *Matronalia*; but the people of Tunbridge Wells might not have
known much about that if the superstition had not been kept alive for
commercial reasons at the Continental spas. Alive to this, Dr. Rowzee,
with his customary astuteness, in announcing the various uses of the Tunbridge water declared that it induced fecundity by enlivening the blood and
'the nobler parts of the body and spirits,' producing in them 'a sweet
balsamick, spirituous and sanguineous temperament; which naturally in-
cites men and women to amorous emotions and titillations, being previous
dispositions enabling them to procreation.' Where doctors wrote so sug-
gestively about the aphrodisiac properties of mere cold water, with a little
mineral in it, we can hardly be surprised to find lesser mortals whispering
in corners. It is said that when Sheridan first imagined *The School for Scandal*
he saw in his mind's eye the opening scene set in the pump-room at Bath,
and we may be sure that the malicious inuendos of Mrs. Candour echoed the
conversation he was accustomed to hear there.

At Bath, much more than at Tunbridge Wells, this indelicate element
was only to be expected, because there the baths were hot, and hot baths
had always been associated with brothels. This was particularly so with
Turkish baths, which some say were introduced into England by the
Crusaders. Ben Jonson refers to these 'hot-houses,' and certainly the
'sweating-baths' of London were the resorts of the most depraved of the
city's characters. As early as Henry II's reign we find regulations for their
control which obviously indicate that they were used for immoral purposes,
and in Henry VIII's reign they were closed altogether as the result of the
alarming spread of venereal disease having been traced to them.

The Cross Bath, as we learn from *A Step to the Bath* (1700), even in the
seventeenth century was much more widely renowned for its pleasures than
ever it was for its cures: 'Here is perform'd,' we are told, 'all the Wanton
Dalliances imaginable; celebrated Beauties, Panting Breasts, and Curious
Shapes, almost Expos'd to Publick View: Languishing eyes, Darting Killing
Glances, Tempting Amorous Postures, attended by soft Musick, enough to

33 'The Little Green Man, or The Bath Bugabo, or the Widows' Terror'

From a satirical print of 1802

34 The Warm Bath

35 The Shower Bath
From illustrations by J. Green, 1813

EAUX DE SCANDAL

provoke a *Vestal* to forbidden Pleasure, Captivate a Saint, and charm a *Jove*: Here was also different Sexes, from *Quality* to the Honourable *Knights*, Country *Put* and City *Madam's*...the ladies with their floating *Jappan* Bowles, freighted with Confectionary, Knick-knacks, Essences and Perfumes, Wade about like Neptun's Courtiers, suppling their Industrious Joynts. The Vigorous Sparks, presenting them with several Antick Postures, as Sailing on their Backs, then Embracing the Element, sink in Rapture ...' It was little wonder that Bath came to be described at one time as 'a Valley of Pleasure, yet a Sink of Iniquity.'

This curious work, *A Step to the Bath*, was issued anonymously; but it is almost certainly the work of Edward, or Ned, Ward, a tavern-keeper whose humorous sketches of social life are not in the best taste, and at times are coarse if not vulgar, but seem to be a perfectly fair picture of low life. In his best known work, *The London Spy*, in which a country visitor is conducted round the sights of London by a cockney acquaintance, the Hummums in Covent Garden are described, and we can see how easily these would degenerate into houses of ill repute. The bathers undressed themselves and were led into the heated chamber, which, says Ward in his vivid style, was 'hot as a pastry cook's oven,' and where the patient soon felt like 'a piece of butter in a basting ladle.' The floor of this chamber was of freestone, and to protect the feet, wooden-soled sandals were worn. Soon the bathers became soaked with perspiration. The Masseur then entered, with a gauntlet of coarse camel's hair on his hand, and curried the bathers as briskly as a Yorkshire groom currying his master's horses. Next, they were wiped clean with calico napkins and put into a hot bath, where they were left to boil out such 'gross humours' as might still be lingering in the body. After this they were wiped again by the attendant, and as by this time the hot baths had made them feel weak and drowsy a bed was provided, on which, to the accompaniment of soft music, they were again, but this time more gently and soothingly, wiped and massaged. Roman history has a good deal to say about the less reputable side of bathing, and Milton condemned the new English habit of taking hot baths because he feared that what had happened in Rome would be repeated here. The *bagnios*, or houses of ill-fame, in Bath were in Avon Street, sometimes referred to as the local Wapping, a district described in *Egan's Walk through Bath*.

But it must not be thought that everyone in England found the spas romantic, and their waters productive of amatory excitement. One lady visitor, who doubtless spoke for many, said she was quite unable to see how a bedraggled appearance in a bath promoted sex appeal, and Hammond, in his *Short Survey of Twenty-Six Counties* says, 'to see young and old, rich and poore, blind and lame, diseas'd and sound, English and French, men and women, boyes and girles, one with another, peepe up in their caps, and appear so nakedly and fearfully, in their uncouth naked postures, would a little astonish and putt one in mind of the Resurrection.'

The man who exposes all the nonsense and humbug of spa life most effectively is dear old grumpy Matthew Bramble in *Humphry Clinker*. There was nothing romantic about the spas for him. Writing to his friend, Dr. Lewis, about Bath, he became as hot as the waters themselves in describing his disgust and boredom—disgust at the sight of so many unhealthy people steeping themselves in the same contaminated water, and boredom with the alleged pleasures of Bath. 'I was persuaded to go to a ball,' he writes, 'on purpose to see Liddy dance a minuet with a young petulant jackanapes, the only son of a wealthy undertaker from London, whose mother lodges in our neighbourhood, and has contracted an acquaintance with Tabby. I sat a couple of long hours, half stifled, in the midst of a noisome crowd; and could not help wondering, that so many hundreds of those that rank as rational creatures, could find entertainment in seeing a succession of insipid animals, describing the same dull figure for a whole evening, on an area, not much bigger than a taylor's shop board. If there had been any beauty, grace, activity, magnificent dress, or variety of any kind, howsoever absurd, to engage the attention, and amuse the fancy, I should not have been surprised; but there was no such object: it was a tiresome repetition of the same languid, frivolous scene, performed by actors that seemed to sleep in all their motions.'

Much of the scandal at the English spas in the late seventeenth century did not amount to anything more than idle gossip about the unrestrained high spirits of a nation set free after years of unnatural control. Love-making, which under the Puritans had been a hole-and-corner business, came out into the open, and for a time the older people were shocked. But in the eighteenth century the root cause of both scandalous conduct and scandalous talk was boredom. Tea was perhaps the real water of scandal. The two always seem to have been taken together. In the time of Queen Anne, and even in that of the early Georges, tea-drinking was something of an indulgence. As the *Bath Miscellany* had it:

> How see we Scandal (for our sex too base),
> Seat in dread Empire in the Female Race,
> 'Mong Beaus and Women, Fans and Mechlin Lace,
> Chief seat of Slander, Ever there we see
> Thick Scandal circulate with right Bohea.

There, source of black'ning Falsehood's Mint of Lies,
Each Dame the'Improvement of her Talent tries,
And at each Sip a Lady's Honour dies;
Truth rare as Silence, or a Negro Swan,
Appears among those Daughters of the Fan.

It was boredom that made gambling so great a curse in the eighteenth-century spas. Indeed it is said that doctors were even known to recommend gambling to their patients in the hope of rousing them from their morbid introspection and chronic lethargy. There was much less domestic life in the eighteenth century than there was in the nineteenth. The men of the well-to-do classes spent their evenings at their clubs, their coffee-houses, the tavern, or the theatre. Except when in the country they seldom stayed at home. The women, on the other hand, were house-bound throughout the winter, and amused themselves with such games as Blindman's Buff, Cross Purposes, Hot Cockles, 'Parson has lost his Cloak,' or such of the fashionable games for clever people as 'Bouts Rimez,' which is described in the *Spectator*, No. 60. Four rhyming words were given to each contestant, and from these, four lines of sensible if uninspired verse had to be made, the lines ending with the rhymes provided. Musical evenings, too, were popular; but everywhere the most familiar sound of the day was the rattle of dice. In *A Step to the Bath* the scene is described: 'From hence we went to the Groom-Porters, where they were labouring like so many Anchor Smiths at the Oakes, Backgammon, Tick Tack, Irish Basset and throwing of Mains. There was Palming, Lodging, Loaded Dice, Levant and Gammoning with all the Speed imaginable; but the Cornish Rook was too hard for them all.' According to Ned Ward's *Adam and Eve stript of their Furbelows*, such a hold had gambling on the fashionable lady of the day that, 'Were she at her Parish Church, in the Height of her Devotion, should any Body in the Interim but stand at the Church Door and hood up the *Knave of Clubs*, she would take it to be a Challenge at *Lanctre Loo*; and starting from her prayers, would follow her beloved *Pam*, as a deluded Traveller does an *Ignis Fatuus*;' They had another game called *One and Thirty*, a very expensive game according to Dean Swift.

Defoe, in his *Tour through England and Wales* (1724-6) says of Bath that the whole of the time is spent in 'a round of the utmost diversion,' and that 'the town is taken up in raffling, gameing, visiting, and in a word, all sorts of gallantry and levity.' Stakes rose so high that in the *Guardian* No. 174 Steele says that the gravity of the players might put one in mind of a council meeting. So serious a business had gaming become that the ladies affected by the fever neglected their looks, threw their features into violent distortions while playing, and lost their complexions by late hours and worry, although for the ladies to neglect their appearance was then, as always, a sad mistake:

> *This Itch for play has likewise fatal been,*
> *And more than Cupid draws the Ladies in,*
> *A Thousand Guineas for Basset prevails,*
> *A bait when Cash runs low, that seldom fails;*
> *And when the Fair One can't the Debt defray*
> *In Sterling Coin, does Sterling Beauty pay.*[1]

Most of the eighteenth-century visitors to the spas were of the newly created leisured class described in the last chapter, and people of infinite leisure are seldom the fortunate creatures they appear to the overworked. In spite of all the advertised delights of the spas, Lord Chesterfield was probably speaking for many besides himself when he wrote to Lord Suffolk in 1737: 'Were it not for the comfort of returning health, I believe I should hang myself; I am so weary of sauntering about, without knowing what to do, or of playing at low-play, which I hate, for the sake of avoiding high, which I love.'

But we cannot believe that such boredom would often affect the young, except, perhaps, those who had no aptitude for love-making, which as an art must have reached its highest degree of technical complexity at the spas. The colour display, which has always been natural in courtship, the coy preliminaries and bold advances of the traditional love-play, became as brilliant and gay between each beau and belle at the spas as between the most lustrously plumaged cock and hen in an aviary. The natural history of courtship is an engaging subject. Each section has both a constant and a variable element, the latter ranging from the whistle of the most vulgar cockney tea-garden to the elaborate and punctiliously observed formalities of Bath. In London the most common custom was to tread on the lady's train, or 'accidentally' cause her some minor embarrassment, then apologise profusely, and if she did not flick her parasol scornfully in the gallant's face and move away haughtily, to suggest tea in one of the arbours of the garden, to be followed in due course by a stroll in the shrubbery.

Then as now, of course, there were a few bold spirits who by-passed the preliminaries. The story goes that a celebrated beauty of George II's time was walking in Marylebone Gardens one day, when a complete stranger strode up to her, slipped his arm round her waist and kissed her. Naturally,

---

[1] Epilogue to *The Gamester*, ed. 1705.

she started back in fear and consternation: 'Don't be alarmed, Madam,' said the bold young man, 'You can now boast that you have been kissed by Dick Turpin.'

In the fashionable spas the most brilliant period of display came after Morning Prayer, when the entire company, except those who went riding, walked on the parades in their best clothes with no other object than to see and be seen. Defoe in his *Tour* has a vivid description of the scene. He says: 'After the appearance is over at the Wells, (where the ladies are all undress'd) and at the chapel, the company go home; and as if it was another species of people, or a collection from another place, you are surpriz'd to see the walks covered with ladies compleatly dress'd and gay to profusion; where rich clothes, jewels, and beauty not to be set out by (but infinitely above) ornament, dazzles the eyes from one end of the range to the other.

'Here you have all the liberty of conversation in the world, and any thing that looks like a gentleman, has an address agreeable, and behaves with decency and good manners, may single out whom he pleases, that does not appear engag'd, and may talk, rally, be merry, and say any decent thing to them; but all this makes no acquaintance, nor is it taken so, or understood to mean so; if a gentleman desires to be more intimate, and enter into any acquaintance particular, he must do it by proper application, not by ordinary meeting on the walks, for the ladies will ask no gentleman there, to go off the walk, or invite any one to their lodgings, except it be a sort of ladies of whom I am not now speaking.'

In this after-chapel parade, dress was of first importance, with head-dress paramount. This became increasingly elaborate until by about 1775 each lady carried on her head an erection of wool, muslin, lawn, net, lace, gauze, and any other flimsy material, bound together with ribbons and flowers, twined about a wire frame that resembled a miniature pagoda, and was certainly devised for the worship of idols. The *New Bath Guide*, which hits off the age so delightfully, says:

> *A cap like a hat*
> *(Which was once a cravat)*
> *Part gracefully plaited and pinned is,*
> *Part stuck upon gauze,*
> *Resembles macaws*
> *And all the fine birds of the Indies.*
>
> *But above all the rest,*
> *A bold Amazon's crest*
> *Waves nodding from shoulder to shoulder;*

At once to surprise
And to ravish all eyes
To frighten and charm the beholder.

In short, head and feather,
And wig altogether,
With wonder and joy would delight ye;
Like the picture I've seen
Of the' adorable queen
Of the beautiful bless'd Otaheite.

At Epsom and Tunbridge this contest in fine apparel became most farcical, because in these for a time rank was set aside as Beau Nash would never allow it to be at Bath. Consequently the ladies began equal, as it were, and only by their finery could they gain an advantage. In the play *Tunbridge Wells* (1678), for example, the alderman's wife says: 'They rail at me already for wearing such rich points upon my petty-coats, and swear they don't become a tradesman's wife.'

The mischievous time of day, as we should expect, came later. From seven in the evenings, when the company again took to the parades, or assembled for dancing on the smooth turf of the bowling green, it was again the custom for any gentleman, as Defoe told us, to engage any lady in conversation without the formality of an introduction. In this evening parade the ladies often wore masks, and might further disguise their persons by wearing also a hood. Thus concealed, they became much more venturesome in exchanging compliments with the men than they would have been if anyone, including the ladies, could have recognised them. In Colley Cibber's *Double Gallant* (1707) Sir Solomon, the jealous husband, says: 'I'll step into the park, and see if I can meet with my hopeful spouse there! I warrant, engaged in some innocent freedom (as she calls it), as walking in a mask, to laugh at the impertinence of fops that don't know her; but 'tis more likely, I'm afraid, a plot to intrigue with those that do.'

After dinner, then,
the sport begins,
Whether your fancy leads to Bowls or Pins.

Of Tunbridge Wells the author of *A Journey through England* (4th ed. 1724) says 'I believe there is no place in the world better to begin an intrigue in than this, nor than London to finish it.' Defoe says plainly 'And yet Tunbridge also is a place in which a lady however virtuous, yet for want of good conduct may as soon shipwreck her character as in any part of England;

and where, when she has once injur'd her reputation, 'tis as hard to restore it; nay, some say no lady ever recover'd her character at Tunbridge, if she first wounded it there.'

In vanity, alas! it has most regretfully to be admitted that the men outstripped the women. At no other time has the English male been so affected and foppish as he was in the eighteenth century in spas, parks, and theatres. Nothing could be more absurd than the way he flourished his snuff-box, and swung his gold-headed cane, as he bowed to his lady, or passed the time of day with a gentleman of his acquaintance. At any moment he might take out a small hand-mirror, such as every beau carried, and proceed to adjust his periwig, or tighten his cravat. In the poem *Islington Wells* his love of flowery language is deservedly ridiculed:

> *For using vulgar words and phrases,*
> *Their mouth most inf'nitely debases,*
> *To say they've melancholy been*
> *Is barbarous; no, they are chagrin.*
> *To say a lady's looks are well*
> *Is common; no, her air is belle.*
> *If anything offends, the wig*
> *Is lost, and they're in such fatigue.*

In every aspect of life at the Georgian spas there was so much conceit and so little sincerity that one cannot help wondering what the love-making for which they were famous was worth. Creatures so much in love with themselves as the gallants, beaux, macaroni, and dandies who succeeded each other in the long procession of posturing and performing males, and in the second procession of simpering, ogling females, cannot have had much heart to give to each other. The novelists of the day set, not their most romantic, but their most absurd love scenes in the spas, and sent to them their least reputable characters for the purposes of courtship. 'When a young Widow,' wrote the Abbé Le Blanc in *Lettres d'un Français,* 'or an elderly Dowager desire to burn incense afresh on the altars of Hymen, it is here they come to sacrifice to the God.' Every romantic artifice and design was cultivated assiduously; but how much reality there was behind the show of affection is not easily determined. Marriages there were; but we may recall how distressed Lydia in Sheridan's play, *The Rivals,* was at the thought of being married without being first abducted. Such a notice as this, taken from the *Bath Chronicle* for the 9th September 1773 is typical of many: 'The honourable Mrs. —, daughter of Lady M—rs, set off from her house near the city in a postchaise and four with Mr. L—, a young gentleman of good family and fortune in Dorsetshire.' We can imagine the excitement such an announcement would cause. But excitement with diminishing flutters. The naughtiness of the spa ladies became as conventional and as boring a joke as that of the Aberdonian miser, and as time went on it came to have as little warrant. Seen across the centuries this love-making at the spas has a curious anthropological interest. At first, as we have seen in connection with Epsom and Tunbridge Wells, social as well as moral conventions were laid aside for a few weeks each season, while Nature regained her sway exactly as she did in the old pagan festivals. Indeed, at this time spa life was, if you like, a last outcrop of paganism and comparable with mediaeval May-Day and Twelfth-Night festivities or Shrovetide fooleries. It was a social safety-valve in an age that was trying desperately hard to keep the old Adam under, but could not yet make up its mind to strangle him. In course of time it became as harmless a pastime as ensnaring a curate. In *Tom Jones*, Partridge, on the arrival of Sophia Western and her maid at the inn at Upton, remarks: 'I warrant neither of them are better then they should be, a couple of Bath trulls, I'll answer for them.' But there is another story, which relates how a lady of fashion on looking back to bid farewell to her beloved city of Bath as she left it, murmured tenderly: 'Farewell, dear Bath, nowhere so much scandal, nowhere so little sin.'

36 Promenaders on the North Parade

From a water-colour by T. Malton, c. 1795

37 The Concert Room

From an aquatint by J. C. Nattes, 1806

BATH

38. Dinsdale Spa, Durham

From an engraving after T. Allom, 1833

39 Gilsland Spa, Cumberland

From an engraving after T. Allom, 1834

NORTHERN SPAS

Chapter Seven

NORTHERN SPAS

Sure of the fortieth spare arm-chair
When gout and glory seat me there.

BROWNING
Dis aliter visum

I. BUXTON

SO far as we know with certainty, Buxton and Bath have the only springs that were used by the Romans for purposes of healing and relaxation. The waters of both are thermal; but those of Bath alone can ever have served for indulgence. Buxton's waters must always have been tonic. Certainly its climate can never have been sedative. Before Science got the better of Nature, surely the only reason that could induce invalids to endure its rigours would be that given by Mrs. Delany in a letter written in 1766 to the Duchess of Portland, who was then having treatment. 'Buxton is a *shocking* place,' ran the consoling line, 'but the blessing of health is worth a state of trial.' When travel was travail, and lodging-house beds hard and lousy, a town set among the bleak forbidding hills of the Peak, a thousand feet above sea-level, can hardly have been enticing. So its waters must then have been thought of only as waters of healing—never of pleasure, to say nothing of scandal. But all that is altered. To-day Buxton is one of the finest and most attractive towns in the North. Scenery that was once thought repellent is now inviting. Good roads, hospitable inns, and the many benefits bestowed on the town by the Dukes of Devonshire have annulled the inconveniences of the region, and made its bold scenery and bracing air as inspiring as they were formerly depressing. The town has an aristocratic air, and it was a happy thought that prompted Sir John Floyer, the eighteenth-century authority on baths, to dedicate his work to the Duke of Devonshire, for, as he said, 'Baths were always thought worthy of the care of statesmen; and Cato opposed the introducing of the use of hot baths in Rome, by which the Roman manners might be corrupted, and their bodies made more effeminate. . . . I hope your Grace will imitate the

85

counsel of this noble patriot, by encouraging this present age to leave off the imprudent use of hot baths, and to regain their ancient natural vigour, strength and hardiness by a frequent use of cold bathing.'

Bath and Buxton are now complementary. That we should think of them together is natural, not only because both go back to Roman times and have thermal springs, but because they have architectural features in common—particularly their crescents—and because both have probably had more royal visitors than any other provincial town not graced with a royal palace.

We know little about Roman Buxton. There is convincing evidence of its use by the legionaries; but no remains of their baths survive. The history of the town as a spa starts about 1570 with George Talbot, 6th Earl of Shrewsbury, whose family had owned the well for more than a hundred years, building a house for the use of bathers. In 1572 Dr. Jones published his famous work, *The Benefit of the Auncient Bathes of Buckstones,* which was dedicated to the earl, and contains that delightful comparison of the waters of Buxton with those of Bath. The water of Bath, he says, is hotter than that of Buxton, 'By reason whereof, it attracteth and dissolveth more speedily; but Buckstone's more sweetly, more delicately, more finely, more daintily, and more temperately.' The work is now extremely rare. It makes charming reading. Bathing is recommended both morning and evening between the beginning of May and the end of September, when the sun is high, 'the misty exhalations being into the second heaven attracted.' The pious doctor begs all who use the bath with hopes of being healed to pray first, 'either in the appointed places or in your chamber, or on the Bath's side.'

This reference to prayer in Dr. Jones's treatise takes us into a different world from that of the Restoration and Regency spas. There was little that was holy in the fashionable watering-place, less of the pilgrim in the average visitor; yet many of the springs, as we saw in considering the London spas, had their origin in the holy wells of the Middle Ages. St. Ann's Well at Buxton was one such. It had been venerated for centuries by the Derbyshire dalesmen until closed by Thomas Cromwell's orders at the Reformation in the hope of destroying belief in the saint's powers. If St. Chad was the Holy Father of Wells, St. Ann was their Holy Mother, and we can imagine the distress of her votaries, many of whose crutches hung in her chapel near the well, probably on a site now covered by the southern extremity of the Crescent, when Cromwell's agent, Sir William Bassett, came to do his master's bidding. That he did it we know from his letter: 'My Lord, I have locked up and sealed the Baths and Wells of Buckston, that none shall enter to wash there till your Lordship's pleasure be further known.' Only by seeing that some remnant of faith in the sacred character of water survived even as late as the end of the seventeenth century can we explain the countryman's continued regard for the old wells. And surely this faith was not unreasonable by any kind of Christian reckoning. When our Essex country parson, Ralph Josselin of Earl's Colne, a Puritan and chaplain in Cromwell's army, set out for Tunbridge Wells in 1675 he wrote in his diary: 'Intend for Tunbridge. God in Mercy be my physitian; the waters are his prepared physick.' Bishop Ken, who held the see of Bath and Wells from 1685 to 1690, composed prayers for 'all persons who came to the Baths for Cure,' in which, addressing the bathers, he begs them 'to take all imaginable Care, that you do not abuse the *Bath*, by any Lasciviousness or Impurity, which may defile your selves, or others,' adding 'Do not think the Baths can do you any good, without God's immediate Blessing on them, for it is God that must first *heal the Waters*, before they can have any virtue to heal you.'

In the very year in which Dr. Jones's work appeared, a special clause in the Poor Law provided that 'Whereas a great number of poor and diseased people do resort to the city of Bath . . . and the town of Buxton . . . for some ease and relief of their diseases at the baths there, and by means thereof the inhabitants of the same city of Bath and town of Buxton are greatly overcharged,' hereafter 'no diseased or impotent poor person living on alms' should be permitted to visit either place unless he first obtained a licence from two Justices of the Peace and arrangements were made for the cost of the visit to be borne by the home parish.[1]

Dr. Jones describes the generous provisions made by the earl for both rich and poor at Buxton. In addition to building houses for the invalids to lodge in, he provided seats round the baths, 'and chimneys for fire, to air your garments in the Bath's side, and other necessaries most decent.' A register was to be kept, and everything connected with the spa was to be conducted in an orderly manner. A scale of charges, based on social not physical condition, and ranging from one shilling for a yeoman to £3-10-0 for a duke and £5-0-0 for an archbishop, had already been fixed.

It was in the earl's 'goodly house, four-square, four storeys high,' adjoining the chief spring that his prisoner, Mary Queen of Scots, stayed for about a month in August to September 1573 and on several later occasions. She was visited there by Burghley in 1575, much to the displeasure of Elizabeth, who suspected a plot against her. It seems fairly certain, however, that Burghley went to Buxton at least in part to drink the waters.

[1] 14 Eliz. c. 5. p 36.

Two years later he repeated the visit, this time with the entire approval of his Sovereign. His 'old crazed body' was again in need of treatment; but he was also in Buxton on the queen's business. Earlier that year Leicester had been in the town. At this time he and the queen were off their heads with love for each other, and it seems probable that Leicester went North to ascertain the views of the Queen of Scots, the Earl of Shrewsbury, and other North Country nobles on their proposed marriage. Burghley's visit was undoubtedly to some extent connected with the same royal aspiration, though again he drank the water, as indeed did Leicester. Evidently one of the Court physicians of the day was recommending Buxton water to his more distinguished patients, for the town had many titled visitors in the fifteen-seventies, and in 1576 there was a strong rumour in circulation that the Court would move to Lord Huntingdon's seat in Leicestershire, 'to the end the water of Buxton might have been daily brought thither for my Lord of Leicester, or any other, to have used.'

What the Earl of Shrewsbury began was completed by the dukes of Devonshire. Bess of Hardwick, who married Shrewsbury for her fourth husband, persuaded her former husband, Sir William Cavendish, by whom she had six children, to sell lands in other parts of the kingdom and establish his family in her native Derbyshire. It was she and Sir William who built the original Chatsworth and became the first Cavendish owners of Buxton. Their son was created Earl of Devonshire by James in 1618. The first duke, the eldest son of the third earl, rebuilt Chatsworth; but the magnificent mansion of to-day is largely the work of the fourth duke. His son, the fifth duke, who is said to have been listless, lethargic, and though a good classical scholar a man wholly without ambition, was responsible for rebuilding the town. In November 1774 he and the duchess visited Lord Rockingham at Wentworth Woodhouse in Yorkshire and saw the alterations being made there by John Carr of York. Here, the duke was convinced, was the very man he wanted for his scheme to rebuild Buxton in so dignified a manner that it would eventually rival Bath, then at the height of its glory, with the Royal Crescent just on the point of completion.

Palladian architecture would appeal to so classical a scholar as the duke. Moreover, Wood had been a Yorkshireman, and John Carr was not only the best living architect in the North of England but the master in the Palladian style, which, incidentally, had found its greatest patron in England in Lord Burlington, the duke's grandfather. A Crescent was therefore inevitable (44). It ought to have been built on higher ground; but unfortunately the more desirable site was not the duke's property, and North Country people are notoriously tenacious of their rights. The duke and his architect may also have had in mind the convenience of invalids. The hills at Bath were bitterly criticised by sickly visitors at this time. The hills at Buxton were almost as steep, and the weather could be merciless. Whatever the combination of reasons, Carr's buildings—namely, the Crescent, built in Doric style and completed in 1786, the Great Stables, the houses at Hall Bank and in the Square—were built close to the baths and wells.

40 Buxton: The Royal Crescent
From a drawing by Randolph Caldecott

The duke was justifiably proud of what he had accomplished, and the duchess was so excited that she wrote to her mother, old Lady Spencer: 'I never saw anything so magnificent as the Crescent . . . tho' it must half ruin one, my spirit makes me delight in the Duke's doing it.' As for the stables, they were on a noble scale. No doubt they were all needed, for a visiting nobleman would bring scores of horses with him. His coaches would need either four or six apiece, and the luggage thought essential by both ladies and gentlemen in those days was a wonder to behold. It was not uncommon, for example, to see ladies moving into their new quarters at the head of a procession of servants bearing cages of monkeys, paroquets, cockatoos, macaws, canaries and turtle doves, as well as heavy cases of clothes, food, and linen. The gentlemen of the day were as particular about their stables as they were about their beds, and far more particular about them than they were about the beds of their servants. Yorkshire was the crack county for horses. The stables at Wentworth Woodhouse were then

7

reputed to be the most magnificent in Europe, and John Carr, as a true-born Yorkshireman with the love of horses in his blood, was never happier than when designing stables. They belonged to the more vigorous life of the Northerner, who looked with scorn on the namby-pamby ways of the South.

The Great Stables at Buxton, later converted into the Devonshire Royal Hospital, surpassed even those at Wentworth Woodhouse. They were built, says Glover in his *History of the County of Derby*, 'on gently rising ground, forming on the outside an irregular polygon, but having a circular area within, sixty yards in diameter; round this is a covered gallery, or rise, where the company take exercise on horseback when the weather renders shelter necessary; the ride, inside the circus, is 160 yards round; on one side of the stables is a spacious repository for carriages.' Three hundred horses could be accommodated in them at once, and there were rooms above for grooms and coachmen. In 1858 the sixth Duke of Devonshire, then believed to be the richest man in England, handed this building over to trustees for conversion into a hospital for the sick and poor. The circular exercising court was given an enormous dome with a span larger than that of St. Peter's in Rome, and little by little John Carr's design was sacrificed as art gave way to science.

It was unfortunate that during the Victorian expansion of Buxton no architect worthy to rank with Carr was employed (43). The Hot Bath Colonnade was designed by Joseph Paxton, at that time the duke's head-gardener, who was knighted after designing the Crystal Palace for the Great Exhibition of 1851. The baths themselves were purchased by the Buxton corporation from the duke in 1902, and since then development has been continuous.

To deal with the scientific side of spa life is no part of the purpose of this book. Buxton's social life developed slowly. It never had a Beau Nash. Not until the Crescent was built did the town gain an assembly-room—and, incidentally, a very fine one; not until 1894 did it have a worthy pump-room, where visitors could meet to discuss the topics of the day and display their finery. Buxton has always been far more an outdoor than an indoor spa, notwithstanding its cold winters. Its pride is in its buildings and its open spaces. The twenty-three acres of gardens along the banks of the river Wye, with the Pavilion near the principal entrance, are now the social centre; but to see the town to best advantage one must climb St. Ann's cliff and look across the opposite slope, with the Crescent at the foot, the Devonshire Royal Hospital on the left, and on the right the Palace Hotel, completed in 1868. But the heart of the region is still out of sight. Since Bess of Hardwick brought her first Cavendish husband to live among the Derbyshire hills Chatsworth has determined the fortunes of Buxton. In the long line of its dukes the most imposing was the sixth, who reigned like a king in Derbyshire for forty-seven years. His coachmen wore wigs, his footmen were powdered, and he himself wore beautifully flowered and embroidered waistcoats long after these adornments had been discarded in other noble households. It was in his honour that the annual well-flowering custom was revived in 1840, to express his tenants' appreciation of the two water fountains he had provided for the village. This festival held annually towards the end of June, with its pageant, fair, old English dancing, and gymkhana, has increased in popularity with each decade until it is now the most important event in the Buxton calendar.

II. MATLOCK

Buxton's neighbouring spa, Matlock Bath (41), one of the group of four Matlocks strewn along the banks of the river Derwent, also has thermal waters. Their temperature is lower than that of Buxton's waters; but they are in high repute, partly because they are so highly charged with radium, partly because they can be taken without stint like common tap-water. Their constant use is held by Derbyshire folk to promote long life and give complete immunity from certain illnesses. Be that as it may, the Matlocks have natural advantages that guarantee their continued popularity, particularly with those who wish to explore the Derbyshire dales. Their climate is much milder than Buxton's, which also means, of course, that it is less bracing. Rocks and cliffs, known in the district as tors, rise so steeply that half way through the dale, in the part where Matlock Bath is situated, the valley becomes a gorge, with houses and hotels perched along the tree smothered cliffs under the Heights of Abraham and the Heights of Jacob (42). Such architects as the Woods of Bath or Carr of Buxton were never needed here. Nature was the architect and man, whether willingly or not, was forced to follow her lines and build where she directed. And Nature was in sportive mood when Matlock Dale was fashioned. Unexpected caverns, streams that suddenly disappear underground, or as suddenly reappear, woods that one moment enclose you and the next open out to reveal unimagined prospects, make scrambling along the moorland tracks behind the villages a most rewarding if somewhat hazardous pursuit.

We know that some of the caverns hereabouts were lead mines worked by the Romans, because pigs of lead bearing Latin inscriptions have been found in the district, and are now in the Derby Museum. They are, however, Matlock's only indisputable link with the Romans. Whether the baths were used by the legionaries or not is a moot point. Roman masonry was discovered round the Old Bath, which was in the grounds of the former Royal Hotel; but it is unlikely that the three medicinal springs here were used before the end of the seventeenth century, when they became known for the cure of 'colic, consumption, gout, chronic rheumatism, and cutaneous cases.' Tuberculosis, I am told, is still unknown in long established Matlock families.

The wells most popular with modern visitors are those with petrifying water, of which there are several near the Royal Pavilion. The explanation of their special property is that rain-water, soaking through the local rock becomes loaded with carbolic acid, which dissolves the limestone and holds it in solution until the stream emerges into the open air. Some of the carbolic acid then escapes and the excess lime is released for deposit. Birds-nests, plants, and curiously shaped objects of every kind are placed in the water until they become encrusted, and are then sold as souvenirs. Ornaments made from an attractive local spar called 'Blue John' are also displayed in the village shops, and these local gifts are interesting in a study of the spas collectively because keepsakes and local crafts have always been associated with popular spas and wishing-wells, most notably, perhaps, at Tunbridge Wells.

Of the other three Matlocks two, the old village and Matlock Bridge, do not come within our scope. They were never spas, though Matlock Bridge is now popular with visitors who prefer a wider sky and more air than they have at the Bath. It is the fourth, Matlock Bank, that through the drive and enterprise of a local hosiery manufacturer, John Smedley, became the first great centre of popular hydropathy in Great Britain. Smedley was a character. To be frank about him, he was a caricature of the typical pig-headed, half-educated small-town mill-owner who, by stupendous faith in himself as the divinely appointed cock of his own dunghill, dominated his particular Lancashire, Yorkshire, or Derbyshire dale during the middle years of the Industrial Revolution. How Dickens would have revelled in him! Throughout his life he waged unceasing warfare on two orders of men whose works he believed were the Devil's own—doctors of medicine and the Anglican clergy. Out of warfare with the former came Smedley's Hydro, the greatest institution of its kind in the kingdom, out of warfare with the second came a flock of pamphlets that in his own generation hooted like owls through the Derbyshire dales, as well as a great number of Nonconformist chapels, in which he preached his fiery 'gospel' every Sunday, denouncing doctors and parsons as 'blind leaders of the blind,' and as 'having the form of

41 The Buildings at the Bath, about 1750
From a Carrington Bowles print

42 Matlock Bath and the River Derwent
From an engraving after W. H. Bartlett, 1842

MATLOCK, DERBYSHIRE

43 A PANORAMA OF BUXTON, about 1850, with the Church and Old Hall Hotel or

From a mid-

44 Buxton: The Crescent, designed by John Carr of York, 1780–84

From an engraving after E. Dayes, 1803

left, the Crescent in the centre, and on the right the Hot Baths and Quadrant
orian print

45 Victorian Harrogate

From an engraving after B. Foster

46 Knaresborough: the Dropping Well

From an eighteenth-century print

47 Harrogate: the New Sulphur Spring

From an engraving after N. Whittock, 1829

godliness, but denying the power thereof.' But the calling of superman is a strain. Smedley boasted that he could do as much work as any two ordinary men, and for a time he did. Then the inevitable breakdown came and he had to rest. There could be no question of calling in a doctor; but he heard of a water-cure at Ben Rhydding and decided to try it. By some means—water, moorland air, rest, the three in combination, or the intervention of Providence, he was restored to health, and suitable services of thanksgiving were offered. But Smedley was not the man to let the matter end there. He could denounce and confound the clergy in his chapels; he now had a 'gospel' that would confound the doctors. So with the zeal of a prophet he went into action. In 1853 he bought a cottage on Matlock Bank where water treatment, under his direction, was already being used, and for the rest of his life poured into the concern so much energy and capital that at his death in 1874 Smedley's ranked with the best hydropathic establishments in the world.

This cold water cure was not new. Indeed it was practised by Hippocrates in the fourth century B.C.; but hydropathy in the modern sense was the latest fad in John Smedley's day. It was not introduced into England until 1840, when Dr. Wilson of Malvern and a Captain Clarige founded their respective homes. One of the first in the movement was Dr. Macleod, who built the Ben Rhydding Hydro where Smedley received his scientific rebirth in 1849.

One trembles to think of the harm John Smedley could have done if the idea had not in the main been sound. The water cure amounted to little more than a nature-cure as Smedley practised it. At first he certainly took grave risks—such as plunging people with fever into tubs of cold water. In the early days he used to send patients to a nearby well in the depth of winter wearing neither shoes nor stockings. The result of such treatment frightened the 'doctor' as well as the patients. We might, in fact, say that it came as near to curing the one as it did to killing the other. Cold, Mr. Smedley concluded, was not good for the feet. But he was equal to this startling discovery. He promptly invented a fur-lined Wellington boot for use in winter and his self-confidence was fully restored.

Apart from his fads, John Smedley was a simple, good-living man who did his best for his workpeople. His heart was in the right place, and he was no fool. After a lifetime of chapel-building, pamphleteering and tilting at windmills, he died worth more than a hundred thousand pounds and left in his hydro a magnificent memorial.

III. HARROGATE

It is a curious coincidence that William Slingsby's discovery of the medicinal spring 'upon a rude barren moore' within the Royal Forest of Knaresborough, which gave rise to the town of Harrogate, should have been made within a few months of the Earl of Shrewbury's establishment of Buxton as a spa. In the second half of the seventeenth century new spas were discovered every year; but in 1571 English spas on the Continental model were unknown. Such medicinal springs as were then in use were holy wells that had survived the Reformation, and the fact that most of them were in the West and North cannot be dissociated from the strength of Catholic resistance in those parts. Harrogate as well as Buxton had its St. Ann's Well; but its best-known holy well was dedicated to St. Mungo, the apostle of the Strathclyde Britons, who flourished in the middle of the sixth century, and was opposite the present Harlow Manor Hotel in Cold Bath Road. The establishment of Harrogate as a spa, however, has very little connection with it. William Slingsby, so far as we know, was not interested in holy wells. His discovery of the Tewit Well, as he called it, is not unlike Lord North's discovery of the Tunbridge well in 1606. With both we have a gentleman 'of ancient and worthy family' passing through a forest and noticing water of peculiar iridescence bubbling up from the ground. Both had visited the Belgian Spa, and both on drinking from the English spring realised that it had properties in common with the Continental. Slingsby, being a Yorkshireman, even thought the Harrogate water better than that of Spa. It was, he said, 'more brisk and lively, and of more speedy operation.' So he had a wall built round the spring, which is now to be found near the south-east extremity of the Stray, the breezy tract of greensward that gives to Harrogate as a spa an air of freedom and spaciousness lacking in those already noticed, where life was so much more restricted and conventional that it could ever be in Yorkshire. The Stray is, in fact, an old grazing common, and appears in early accounts of the town as 'the Stinted Pasture.' When in 1841 the Royal Pump Room was erected over the sulphur well, and a smaller pump-room over the Sweet Spa, or John's Well, the dome from the former was set up over the Tewit Well and serves to give it the prominence it is entitled to as Harrogate's original well.

Twenty-five years later Dr. Timothy Bright referred to Mr. Slingsby's well as 'The English Spa,' and in doing so introduced a new noun into the language. Thus, by assuming in 1596 the name that was subsequently conferred on all watering-places with mineral wells, Harrogate has grounds for claiming to be the first of our national spas.

The first treatise on its waters came in 1626 with the publication of Dr. Deane's *Spandarine Anglica*; or *The English Spaw Fountain*, 'being a brief treatise of the acid, or tart fountain in the Forest of Knaresborough, in the West-Riding of Yorkshire, as also a relation of other medicinal waters in the said Forest.' With true Yorkshire acumen Dr. Deane, not altogether truthfully, warned his readers that the water must not be carried away for consumption elsewhere or its special virtues would be lost. Later, when spa waters were being bottled and offered for sale in London, this traffic was opposed both violently and ingeniously by doctors and innkeepers, who saw that for them the hour had struck if their elaborate and expensive cures were reduced to a case of threepenny bottles from a Bayswater shop. Dr. Deane, therefore, must be regarded as a great benefactor to his profession for having observed that as much powder of galls as would lie on a silver two-penny piece would turn a glassful of spa-water claret colour on the spot, in York would produce but a faint purple, and twenty miles farther away would have no recognisable effect whatever. Unfortunately Yorkshire candour was to over-rule Yorkshire astuteness, when Dr. Garnett, another physician who wrote on the Harrogate, or Knaresborough water, as it was then called, said he had found that if well corked and sealed it could be kept for three or four days without blushing any less rosily when confronted with either tincture of galls or prussian alkali.

The doctors also differed, though less radically, in their opinion of how much water a patient ought to drink. Dr. Deane prescribed up to five pints daily. Dr. Garnett did not expect his patients to be quite so pot-valiant as that, but he thought they would have to drink it in considerable quantities if they expected it to be effective. Happily, the Tewit well was still the favourite, so it was not water from the sulphur wells, on which Harrogate's subsequent fame was to depend, that had to be suffered. The next doctor-author to preach the new doctrine of regeneration by water—applied internally—was Dr. Stanhope, whose work (1632) bore on its title-page the legend: 'Cures without Care, or a summons to all such as find little or no help by the use of physic, to repair to the Northern-Spaw; wherein, by many precedents of a few late years, it is proved to the world, that infirmities, of their own nature desperate, and of long continuance, have received perfect cure, by virtue of mineral waters, near Knaresborough, in the West-Riding of Yorkshire.'

By the middle of the seventeenth century a sulphur well had come into use at Harrogate, and in the second half of the century we have a succession of distinguished visitors writing their impressions of these Yorkshire waters. John Ray, the naturalist, was there in 1661, and wrote in his diary: 'We went to the Spaw at Harrigate and drunk the water. It is not unpleasant to the taste, somewhat acid and vitriolick. Then we visited the sulphur well, whose water, though it be pellucid enough, yet stinks noisomely, like rotten eggs.' From this time forward Harrogate, already firmly established, was able to avail itself to the full of the rising popularity of spas in general. Thomas Amory, in the *Life of John Buncle, Esq.* (1756-66), says of it: 'Of all the watering-places I know, Harrogate is, in my opinion, the most charming. The waters are incomparable; no air can be better; and with the greatest civility, cheerfulness, and good humour, there is a certain rural plainness and freedom mixed, which are vastly pleasing. The lady of pleasure, the well-drest tailor, and the gamester, are not to be found there. Gentlemen of the country, and women of birth and fortune, their wives, sisters, and daughters, are for the most part of the company. There were at least four-score ladies in the country dances every evening while I was there; and amongst them many fine women.' In this passage Amory gives us the clue to the distinctive character of Harrogate as a spa. It was never to attract the ladies of pleasure, the fops and gamesters who frequented the southern spas. It was the resort of the landed families of the North, country squires from the old stone granges of the Yorkshire dales, and the moors and fells farther north, who came to tone up their constitutions with a few weeks in the bracing air of Harrogate, and, if their joints were beginning to creak, to undergo a course at the baths before returning to manage their estates—to sit on their benches, bully their parsons, ride to hounds and drink their pints with their tenant-farmers of an evening.

Meanwhile the growth of the spa continued (46). An Act of Parliament permitting the enclosure of Knaresborough Forest in 1770 made provision for 'certain wells or springs of medicinal waters, commonly called Harrogate Spaws, to which during the summer season great numbers of persons constantly resort.' Two hundred acres of land surrounding the springs were to be preserved as an open space in which no one at any time should sink a pit, work a mine, or do anything harmful to the springs or distasteful to those who used them. But for all this, Harrogate must have remained a small straggling village on what Smollett described as 'a wild common, bare and bleak, without any signs of cultivation,' until in 1786 Lord Loughborough, who built Wedderburn House in that year, began to plant trees on his Wedderburn estate, along the south side of the Stray.

Social life, too, would be vigorous rather than elegant. The country squires already referred to were a fine breed; but they belonged to a rough and ready world. When the weather was not too severe they went indoors only to eat, drink, and sleep. And how they did eat! Here as in nothing else did the Yorkshire spas surpass all their rivals. Even Dr. Deane in 1626 has a glorious description of all the food to be enjoyed at Harrogate, but in a charming passage warns his readers against excessive indulgence: Let the drinkers, he says, be moderate with meat and drink, choosing 'those which are of light and easy digestion, and of good and wholesome nourishment, breeding laudable juice,' and avoiding such as 'beget crude and ill humours.' In one thing, however, Dr. Deane was anything but wise. He discouraged the eating of fruit and vegetables at a time when half the digestive troubles of the people were due to consuming excessive beef, and insufficient greens and fruits. Nevertheless, though this was recognised as a fault in English diet by foreigners, we find Dr. Wittie, fifty years later, disapproving of salads.

As with other resorts, accounts of Harrogate life vary considerably according to the taste of the visitor. Dr. Carlyle, in his *Autobiography* (p. 434), describes the town as having the best company at the least expense of any watering-place in the kingdom. The Scots, with whom it has always been much in favour, had used it in recent years as a 'half-way stop' between Edinburgh and London. They were there in force each season, and no doubt helped to keep the prices down. Breakfast could be had at a mere two-pence apiece for muffins, because it was the custom for the ladies to bring their own tea and sugar. Dinner was a shilling; supper sixpence; and chambers free. Afternoon tea was given by the ladies in turns, which, says Dr. Carlyle, coming but once in four or five weeks was not a serious imposition. That lodgings were free is particularly interesting because it was an old Scots and North of England custom to offer hospitality to travellers. In the first chapter of *St. Ronan's Well*, Sir Walter Scott says in a footnote: 'A charge for lodging, fire, and candle, was long a thing unheard of in Scotland.' Northern heartiness seems to have prevailed everywhere, for every account of the company to be met with at Harrogate agrees that it was much friendlier than at the southern spas, in spite of the fact that confirmed valetudinarians would meet the same people in all the watering-places. Jerry Melford in *Humphry Clinker* says of it: 'At present, the company is more agreeable than one could expect from an accidental assemblage of persons, who are utter strangers to one another. There seems to be a general disposition among us to maintain good fellowship, and promote the purposes of humanity, in favour of those who come hither on the score of health.'

Matthew Bramble, as we should expect, saw the whole set-up through very different spectacles. 'The people who come to drink the water,' he says, 'are crowded together in paltry inns, where the few tolerable rooms

8

are monopolised by the friends and favourites of the house, and all the rest of the lodgers are obliged to put up with dirty holes, where there is neither space, air, nor convenience.' Though the month was June his bed needed the warming pan every night, and as for the water, he disagrees with John Ray in comparing it with rotten eggs. To him it was exactly like bilge water.

Bramble's description of the baths might be thought prejudiced. He says: 'I was conducted into a dark hole on the ground floor, where the tub smoaked and stunk like the pot of Acheron, in one corner, and in another stood a dirty bed provided with thick blankets, in which I was to sweat after coming out of the bath. My heart seemed to die within me when I entered this dismal bagnio, and found my brain assaulted by such insufferable effluvia.... After having endured all but real suffocation for above a quarter of an hour in the tub, I was moved to the bed and wrapped in blankets. There I lay a full hour panting with intolerable heat.' But before we dismiss this as more of poor old Matthew's crotchety humour we must glance at what Dr. William Alexander said in his *Plain and Easy Directions for the Use of Harrogate Waters*. Of this sweating bed, into which the bather was put when he came out of the bath, with two blankets below and three or four above his already overheated body, the doctor says: 'I would advise all those who intend to go through this process, only to sit down five minutes, and consider, that they are going not only into the same bed, but into the very blankets, where hundreds have lain before them, and where hundreds have not only lain, but sweated; that these blankets must be filled with that sweat; and that it did not arise always from sound and healthful bodies, but from bodies diseased both internally and externally: and if, after these reflections, they can calmly lie down in it, they must have little delicacy.'

The tubs Matthew Bramble refers to were long narrow contraptions, rather like coffins in shape. Many writers have described them. Mrs. Hofland, in *A Season in Harrogate* (1811) says:

> Astonished I saw when I came to my doffing,
> A tub of hot water made just like a coffin,
> In which the good woman who attended the bath,
> Declar'd I must lie down as straight as a lath,
> Just keeping my face above water, that so
> I might better inhale the fine fumes from below.
> 'But mistress,' quoth I, in a trembling condition,
> 'I hope you'll allow me one small requisition.

Since scrophula, leporasy, herpes and scurvy,
Have all in this coffin been roll'd topsy turvy;
In a physical sense I presume it is meet,
Each guest should be wrapped in a clean winding sheet ?'
'Oh, no! my good sir; for whatever's your care,
You never can catch anything bad in this air;
And that being settled on solid foundation,
We Harrogate bath-women spurn innovation.'
So cavelier like I submitted to power,
And was coddled in troth for the third of an hour.

Religion counted for little in Harrogate at this time. Not until 1734 was money collected for a chapel-of-ease here, and six more years went by before it was ready for use. Eating and drinking were the most serious indoor pursuits, with dancing and card-playing as occasional pastimes. In 1788 a theatre was built to replace the old barn behind the Granby Arms, which had hitherto served that purpose. It failed, however, and was converted into Mansfield House. A venture that might have been thought sure to succeed, a race-course, opened on the Stray in 1793, also came to nothing. The most flourishing concerns in Harrogate then as always were the inns, particularly the Granby Arms, the Green Dragon, and the Crown. The waters, apparently, provided the appetite, and the landlords of these three houses appeased it. The scene at table must have been a tonic to all but the misanthropic. There were no small tables for separate groups of guests in those days—such as there are in ours, when a request for a table to accommodate a reasonably sized party puts a head-waiter to confusion and throws the room into disorder. Everyone present sat round one large table, with the host at the head to carve the joint in the best tradition of English hospitality. Each house had a weekly ball, and guests at any one inn might attend functions at the other two. Of the three, the Crown was the least sociable, though not through any lack of goodwill on the part of its landlord. It was situated nearer the wells than the other two, and for this reason was more in favour with invalids and elderly people less frivolously inclined than the patrons of the Granby Arms and the Green Dragon were wont to be in days when the former was known locally as the House of Lords, and the latter as the House of Commons.

Modern bathing facilities were not provided in Harrogate until 1832, when John Williams built the first Victorian Baths near the Town Hall in Low Harrogate. The Harrogate of to-day is distinctively a nineteenth-century town. Perhaps the man to whom it owed most of its later prosperity was Joseph Thackwray, a member of the family that produced the novelist, whose forbears came from Hampsthwaite. The Harrogate Thackwrays, or Thackerays, owned the Crown Hotel for several generations and were leading citizens. For the convenience of his guests, the Joseph Thackwray who was there in the 1830s sank a well in his own cellar; but as this was said to be harmful to the old sulphur well nearby he was indicted under the provisions of the Knaresborough Enclosure Act. But Joseph Thackwray was not the man to be beaten. When the case came up for trial at York Assizes on the 14th March 1837 he said that he was willing to allow the public free access to the well, and the case was thereupon dismissed. Unfortunately, Mr. Thackwray did not live to derive the benefit he expected from the patrons of his new well—expected because although the water was to be free, he knew that the drinkers would soon want something to take away the taste, and that something he was licensed to supply. He died within a few weeks of his appearance in court.

This mid-nineteenth-century Harrogate (45) is amusingly described for us in a small book published in 1841 entitled *Sketches of Harrogate,* by A Citizen of the World. 'Most of the visitors,' we learn, 'are early risers. At seven o'clock, or soon after, they flock down to the Old Sulphur Well, the waters of which are distributed by some eight or ten nymphs, whose personal attractions are not calculated to make one insensible to the nauseous flavour of the draught which they bestow. The lady paramount of the fount is an old dame, styled indifferently 'Old Betty,' and 'The Queen of Harrogate,' over whose head some eighty summers have passed, without diminishing her activity or garrulity. She is a privileged person, and dispenses the waters and quips and quodlibets with equal liberality. It is curious to observe the various effects which these draughts produce upon the countenances of those who partake of them. Disgust is expressed in a thousand ludicrous ways. . . . The scene is not infrequently heightened by the very unsophisticated exclamations of some burly novice from the wilds of Yorkshire, or the classic districts of Bolton, Oldham, &c, who imbibes the waters for the first time.' The scene of this comedy would be under the dome that now covers the Tewit Well.

With the building of the Royal Pump Room over the old sulphur well in 1841, of a smaller pump-room over the Sweet Spa, or John's Well, on the Stray—which took its name from an attendant named John Hardcastle, who lived to be ninety-six[1]—and the extension of the beautiful gardens originally planted by Mr. Thackwray of the Crown, Harrogate came to the fore as a prosperous inland resort. To-day it is yet one more claimant to the

[1] A previous attendant, William Westmorland, had lived to be 99.

48 SCARBOROUGH from the Spa, about 1835

From an engraving by H. B. Carter

49 Scarborough: The Spa in 1813
From an illustration by J. Green

title of Queen of Watering-places. Apparently, in the number and quality of these fair resorts, England has more queens than even Henry VIII possessed. Some, it may be added, were as short-lived. But Harrogate was particularly well placed for success. From the point of view of its waters, it has more than eighty springs which, though rising within the compass of a few acres, are all different in their chemical constitution. Bogs Field alone, now part of the Valley Gardens, has a greater variety of waters than have yet been found in a similar space anywhere else in the world.

The reason for this curious phenomenon is geological. Harrogate lies at the end of an anticlinal axis running north-eastward from a point on the Lancashire-Yorkshire border near Clitheroe. This range of hills breaks abruptly in what is known as the Harrogate Fault, thus allowing the water to rise through the interstices of the up-tilted strata, the rock keeping the different springs apart. It is as though these eighty-six springs had come up to the earth's surface through eighty-six separate pipes.

The reasons for Harrogate's social success are no doubt many and varied; but probably the most important is its proximity to the great manufacturing towns of Yorkshire. If its first character as a spa was determined by the Yorkshire squires and their ladies who put up for a few weeks at the Granby Arms and the Green Dragon, its character to-day is determined by the tastes of the manufacturers and merchants who, since the Industrial Revolution, have progressively displaced the gentry in the gardens and pump-rooms, as well as in such august assemblies as those of the Granby Arms.

IV. SCARBOROUGH

The same hearty English life—and Yorkshire life at that—which made Harrogate the favourite resort in the eighteenth century of the foxhunting squires and parsons of the North was to be enjoyed at Scarborough (48):

> *Let me put in my Lot at the 'Globe,' or 'New Inn,'*
> *Where the brightest Assemblies of Ladies are seen;*
> *Here on ten modish Dishes, or more to a filling,*
> *I can dine with my Lord, or his Grace for a shilling.*
> *Then soon as from Table the Dinner re-passes,*
> *The bottle goes round, and we toast in full Glasses.*

Dr. Wittie, the first historian of the Scarborough Spa, tells us that the water was discovered about 1626 by a Mrs. Farrow, a 'gentlewoman of good repute who lived in the town.' It is the old story. While walking near the well she noticed that the water stained the stones, and on tasting found it somewhat acid to the palate. So, 'being a discreet Gentlewoman, and also Physically addicted, she thought it probable to have some medicinal quality, and thereupon did both try it herself, and persuaded others that were sickly to drink of it.' Within a few years its fame reached London:

> Let Epsom, Tunbridge, Barnet, Knaresborough be
> In what request they will, Scarborough for me.

Dr. Wittie advanced the claims of the new spa by pointing out that before the Flood, in days when water was the universal drink, men lived for almost a thousand years, whereas after the supposed invention of wine by Noah the span of life was reduced to one tenth. So much of water in general; of the Scarborough water in particular, it was, said Dr. Wittie, highly to be recommended for apoplexy, epilepsy, catalepsy, and vertigo. It cleansed the stomach, opened the lungs, cured asthma and scurvy, black and yellow jaundice, and was a 'Most Sovereign remedy against Hypochondriack Melancholly and Windiness'—against everything, apparently, except long-windedness.

But there was a local doctor named Simpson who was not convinced by his rival. He disputed Wittie's analysis, was so churlish as to drag into the argument several ailments for which the Scarborough waters were not curative, and disparaged the doctor's findings generally. But he gave away his case by showing only too clearly that he was not disinterested in his observations. He was out to advertise 'the Sweet Spaw at Knaresborough [Harrogate] and the Sulphur Well.' In Hydrologia Chimica (1669) Dr. Wittie trounced his critic for an upstart whose words were stuffed with bombast, and who crowed like a cockerell newly hatched from its shell. 'Methinks,' said the older doctor, 'he might have staid till his beard had been grown.'

But that was not the end. If a fight is started in Yorkshire you may be sure that the quarrel will not remain private. The following year Dr. Tunstall flung down another challenge in Scarbrough Spaw Spagyrically Anatomized, to which the doughty Dr. Wittie replied in Scarbrough's Spagyrical Anatomizer Dissected. And still the battle raged. Tunstall returned with The Dissector Anatomized, Simpson with Hydrological Essayes.[1] There seemed to be no limit to the scope of their discussions. Why, they even raised the question of what kind of salt Lot's wife was turned into. Nobody, of course, suffered from all this angry pamphleteering, least of all the doctors themselves. Publicity was as potent then as now, and Dr. Wittie's book was nicely timed. The star of the Yorkshire spas was in the ascendant. More people

[1] See The History of Scarborough, by Arthur Rowntree, chap. VIII, and The History of Mineral Waters, by Dr. Thomas Short, 1734.

were taking to the roads and exploring their native England. We can turn up one another of the well-known travellers of the age, and we find that most of them called at Scarborough. Celia Fiennes, for example, arrived from Agnes Burton, crossing the wolds in a thick mist. 'Scarborough,' she says, 'is a very pretty Sea-port town built on the side of a high hill.' She described the church, the castle ruins, and the harbour, which was secured by 'a mole or halfe moone, two, one within the other, something resembling the Cobb at Lime [Lyme Regis, Dorset].' She tells us that the spa well was on the sands, and that the sea washed into it at high tide, giving its waters a brackish, salty flavour. Then, with a saltiness of her own, she describes a Quaker meeting she attended, remarking tartly that all the prayers were in the first person singular!

Ralph Thoresby, the Yorkshire antiquary, was there in November 1682, and, while interested in the waters, he had useful comments on the town generally. He reckoned, for example, that the castle grounds would provide enough pasture to summer twenty cows. More to our point is an entry in the manuscript diary of Richard Du Cane, junior (1726-29), now in the Essex Record Office:

'Tuesday, 25th October 1726: This morning left Bridlington at nine in our coach and four. We passed very bad roads. Came to Scarborough in six hours and a half, computed twelve miles. This is a very open country. When we came near the town the road lay through a valley of high mountains. Lodged at the New Inn.

Wednesday, 26th October: This morning went to the Spaw, which was built by Richard Dickinson and now kept by him. He is a very deformed man. From thence to the Castle, which is very large and high. Also we were in the Church, which is very large; but when the Castle was battered, some of that was beat down in Oliver's time.'

This same Dickinson is described in a passage quoted by Mr. Arthur Rowntree in his admirable history of the town for which his family has done so much. It is taken from a letter written by a gentleman in Scarborough to his friend in London. Dickinson is called by his local name of Dicky, and is said to be 'one of the most deformed Pieces of Mortality I ever saw, and of most uncouth manner of speech.' This local worthy, we learn, built two houses for visitors: 'The Custom is, as soon as you enter the Room, to subscribe your name in Dicky's Book, and pay Five Shillings ... It is the Custom, for not only the gentlemen, but the ladies also, to bath in the Sea: The gentlemen go out a little way to Sea in Boats (call'd here Cobbles) and jump in naked directly.... The Ladies have the Conveniency of Gowns and Guides.' Under these conditions we are not surprised to hear that when Sarah Duchess of Marlborough visited the spa in 1732 she was very critical of the sanitary arrangements being so public, and retired as quickly as she could for fear she might be obliged to use them!

Nevertheless, in course of time the amenities of Scarborough came to equal those in any other spa, with the typical North Country distinction that outdoor amusements were better catered for than indoor. Mr. Schofield, Scarborough's bookseller-historian in these palmy days, who was clearly a man of parts, gives a vivid picture of gay and lively trains of horse riders galloping across the firm sands each morning, commenting that where in other towns a treaty of marriage might be said to be *afoot*, in Scarborough it was more likely to be *on horseback*, for here, 'as in the times of antient chivalry, a knight, or an esquire, is considered as appearing nowhere more manly, or more acceptable, in the eye of his fair "Lady Love," than on a handsome, well caparisoned steed, obsequiously ready to escort and attend, wheresoever her pleasure may direct the route.'

Mr. Schofield's shop was itself one of the fashionable centres of the town, and probably the most civilising, though Scarborough had another superior shopkeeper at this time whose name was frequently on the lips of visitors: Nanny Salmon, a lady of good family, who till well past her eightieth year kept a curio shop in the town and was the delight of all who knew her.

As at Harrogate, the inns were famous. The chief were the 'New Inn,' the 'New Globe,' the 'Blacksmith's Arms,' the 'Crown and Sceptre,' and the 'Old Globe.' At any of these a man could sit down whenever he pleased to ten or a dozen dishes. The local people could hold their own with the best as cooks, but like all the principal spas Scarborough had London trades- men settled in it for the season. In the seventeen-thirties its life became so polite that Long-room street was often referred to as the Pall Mall of Scarborough, and it was no wonder that Colley Cibber, the laureate who spent so much of his time at Tunbridge Wells, visited the town annually:

> . . . the laurell'd Bard of Britain's King,
> Year after Year, revisits Scarborough's Spring.
> Drinks deep his Draught, and purges well his Brains,
> And from inspiring Water tunes his Strains.

In view of such popularity we can imagine the alarm there was when, in December 1737, a landslide near the spa blocked the spring. Workmen were put on the site at once and clawed the ground with their mattocks like dogs scratching for bones until, to everyone's delight, the stream gushed forth again. But it was not until 1739 that the spa could be reopened. After that it continued to prosper, and when Sheridan's *Trip to Scarborough* went on the boards at Drury Lane in 1777 Lord Foppington was made to exclaim: 'Strike me dumb! Even the boors of this northern spa have learned the respect due to a title.'

The Promenade.

50 *From a drawing by Randolph Caldecott*

Chapter Eight

MIDLAND SPAS

From pangs arthritic that infest the toe
Of libertine excess.

COWPER
The Task, 1. 105-6.

I. MALVERN

THE Midland spas were established as resorts much later than their southern and northern rivals. That all had springs used by the country folk from time immemorial is not in dispute. So, as we shall see later, had hundreds of other towns and villages. Not one in ten of the ancient wells used for healing at some time in their history ever became fully fledged resorts, with the distinctive characteristics we now associate with the name of spa. To refer to these favoured ones as fully fledged is not, perhaps, inappropriate, for they flourished far more on the strength of their metaphorical feathers than ever they did on the intrinsic value of their waters. Malvern, the Worcestershire spa, is an example. Its waters deserve all the praise that has been lavished on them—for their purity, but purity is not what we require of medicinal waters. The mineral properties that might be expected from spa waters these have never possessed. Nor have such properties ever been claimed for them. The water for Malvern's brine baths comes from Droitwich.

But the Malverns, a group of villages spread across the slopes of the Malvern Hills, with the parent town of Great Malvern as their focal point, could not fail to develop as a spa once the social and scenic qualities of such places had been agreed upon. The romantic chain of hills, peaked and sharply featured, extending for nine miles or more, and rising in the Worcestershire Beacon to a height of 1396 feet, provides a perfect setting for an inland watering-place. From the many hotels on the lower slopes visitors can see across Worcestershire on the east, or Herefordshire on the west, and can climb with ease to higher points from which they can see two of the finest landscapes in Britain, the one extending to the Cotswolds, the other to the

Welsh mountains. In the valleys below lie some of England's most endearing market towns, such as Ledbury and Tewkesbury, with Worcester, Gloucester, and Hereford cathedrals within easy reach.

The appearance of these hills is due to their volcanic origin. Sir James Dawson, Principal of the McGill University at Montreal, in his presidential address to the British Association in 1881, said that in his opinion the Malvern Hills were the oldest land in Britain, and probably older than any mountain range in Europe. That is why the waters that rise from them are so pure. They spring from igneous rock, formed at a great depth under volcanic heat and thrust upwards by an earthquake. There are no other hills in the west of England like them, and we can understand Byron, while staying as a boy with his mother at Cheltenham, climbing the Cotswolds to get a view of the Malvern Hills because they reminded him of the Highlands he pined for.

It is very difficult to be sure which is the original well in a spa where there are several that have obviously been used for centuries. John Chambers, in his *History of Malvern*, says this honour goes to what was called Ditchford's Well, about five hundred yards from Little Malvern Church. It was also called Mary's and Nancy's Well, from the names of two women who used to carry its water in bottles for sale at Worcester market, travelling on horseback. What is certain is that the oldest wells used for healing would be those rising on the eastern slopes, because the springs that broke towards the rising sun were always believed to be the purest. Milton, in *Samson Agonistes*, says:

> *Wherever fountain or fresh current flowed*
> *Against the eastern ray, translucent, pure,*
> *With touch ethereal of Heaven's fiery rod,*
> *I drank, from the clear milky juice allaying*
> *Thirst, and refreshed; nor envied them the grape*
> *Whose heads that turbulent liquor fills with fumes.*

So we may assume that St. Ann's Well (51) and Holy Well would be in high repute from an early date.

The town of Great Malvern derives its dignity from the priory church of St. Mary the Virgin and St. Michael, with its noble embattled tower, its Norman nave, its beautiful fourteenth- and fifteenth-century glass and finely carved misericords. Of particular interest are the locally made encaustic tiles in the chancel. There are about a thousand of them. At the Dissolution, Bishop Latimer of Worcester pleaded for the retention of Malvern Priory as a College. It was a well-conducted house, with a prior 'much commended in these parts . . . for he feedeth many, and that daily, for the country is poor and full of penury.' But there was no reprieve. The priory passed into the possession of John Knotsford, sergeant-at-arms, who has a fine alabaster tomb in the church, between the chancel and the chapel of St. Ursula.

The stone for the priory came from a quarry near Bewdley, and doubtless at the Dissolution would be used for John Knotsford's new houses. The priory itself would be a quarry, just as Nonsuch Palace was for the builders of Epsom. To-day the only relic of the priory buildings, apart from the church, is the fifteenth-century gatehouse, constructed of brick faced with sandstone, which spans Abbey Road.

Nothing is heard of the waters being used for curative purposes until a vicar of Malvern in James I's reign made them a subject for thanksgiving in verse; but he mentions only the usual ulcers and bruises, which we hear about in connection with all the mediaeval holy wells. Bad diet, filth, and rough living made these complaints common, and a wash of clear water was often the best ointment. What is interesting, however, is that he says Malvern waters were already being sent hundreds of miles:

> *Some of them into Kent,*
> *Some are to London sent,*
> *Others to Berwick went,*
> *Oh, praise the Lord!*

Evelyn says that in 1654 he 'deviated to the Holy Wells, trickling out of a valley through a steep declivity towards the foot of the great Malvern Hills,' and adds: 'they are said to heal many infirmities, as King's evil, leprosy, sore eyes, etc.' A further reference is to be found in the first volume of the Royal Society's *Philosophical Transactions*, 17th December 1666, where the spring is said to have 'a long and old fame for healing of eyes,' which again was common to most holy wells.

Malvern's development as a town would first be made possible by the disafforestation of the old royal Chase, and the consequent lifting of the great burden of the oppressive forest laws, in the time of Charles I. Then it was that the valley came into cultivation. But there was no spectacular development until the eighteenth century. The man who thought he would transform the scene was a certain William Williams, who was led by the glitter of mica in the syenitic rock to believe that gold might be found there. He sank a mine, but after ten years of fruitless labour abandoned the project in despair. The man who did transform the scene, and indeed who created the Malvern we know, was John Wall, born at Worcester in 1708, who

51 St. Ann's Well

52 The Chalybeate Spa

Both from lithographs by W. H. Wood

MALVERN, ABOUT 1835

53 Leamington Spa: The Royal Pump Room and Baths, about 1820

From an aquatint after W. Rider

54 Low Harrogate: The Spa Well in 1829

From a lithograph by J. Stubbs

after qualifying as a doctor of medicine settled in his native city and became the leading physician in the county. Wall was a man of gifts. He was competent in his own profession, and at the same time an accomplished artist. The passion of his life was his devotion to his native county. He was also a man of enterprise. Spas, as he well knew, were being established in various parts of the kingdom. Why, he must have asked, should there not be one at Malvern, for he analysed the water and published his findings in a tract, which for all its fine language did not disguise the truth that the result was negative. In the words of a local wag:

> *The Malvern water, says Dr. Wall,*
> *Is famed for containing just nothing at all.*

Fortunately the doctor discovered another well, rising from the sandstone of the lower slope, which was at least mildly chalybeate (52). But if there was little here for the scientist in Dr. Wall to work on, there was plenty for the artist. He went ahead with his scheme to turn Malvern into a spa, cutting paths along the slopes, particularly at Malvern Wells. He built boarding-houses and 'honeymoon hotels' for the young people of that romantic age, and sang the praises of the hills on every possible occasion. He was indeed as much the creator of Malvern as Smedley was the creator of Matlock, but was, of course, a much more cultured and likeable man.

Malvern Wells, if it had the grace to remember him, would be sufficient memorial; but it was also Dr. Wall who started the manufacture of Worcester china. He was a Whig, and was therefore frequently in conflict with the dean and chapter of the cathedral, who were Jacobites. The doctor saw that the city was under cathedral control, largely because in most local affairs the dean and chapter paid the piper. So in 1751 he founded the manufacture of Worcester china and became a rival employer of labour, paying good wages to men whom he hoped to interest eventually in the Whig cause. On one occasion Mr. Gladstone, in a speech at the Athenaeum, commented on this remarkable case of an important business being founded for a political motive. Once again, it was the artist in Dr. Wall that led to the new porcelain being so excellent both in colour and design. So while little is heard to-day about Dr. Wall's connection with Malvern waters, Old Worcester is still commended as showing 'Dr. Wall's blue.'

Perhaps the most important date for Malvern in the nineteenth century was 1831, when Princess Victoria, then twelve years old, came with her mother, the Duchess of Kent, to stay at Hollymount Cottage. They spent their time much as they had done at Tunbridge Wells, and the two spas were then at a similar stage of development, which for the princess, perhaps, meant first that there were the same donkey rides in both. But at Malvern there were also the donkey women, with their picturesque bonnets and red cloaks, who made regular trips to St. Ann's Well for the convenience of the gouty and elderly who wished to drink the water. The Princess and her mother stayed for several months, and their visit completed what Dr. Wall had begun. Malvern was now a fashionable watering-place, enjoying the favour of royal patronage. The town never forgot the honour of this visit, and the Jubilee in 1895 was commemorated by the erection of the toposcope that crowns the Worcestershire Beacon.

But fame has its price. About the middle of the nineteenth century Malvern got a succession of water cranks—doctors who founded expensive hydropathic establishments and charged large fees for treatment in which the only part that mattered was diet and exercise. Most of the Malvern we see to-day was built at this time. Enormous hotels such as Dr. Wall never dreamt of went up. Old parts of the town were sacrificed to cater for the thousands of overfed visitors who poured in for a few weeks each season. In 1849, by an act of vandalism, one of its most historic buildings was demolished. This was the great Guesten Hall, a fine and spacious fifteenth-century building in which, no doubt, Sir Reginald Bray, Malvern's first rich benefactor, and his Sovereign, Henry VII, fared sumptuously on venison from the nearby Chase as the prior's guests. The Abbey Hotel, Knotsford, and Abbeyfold were built on the site. It was not an inspiring time to prosper in; but there was much in the Victorian age that was good and sound. A later generation than ours may develop a taste for it, and if it does so Malvern will come into its own again. In the meantime its schools and colleges have made it well known as an educational centre, and the Malvern Festival, the annual dramatic event started by Sir Barry Jackson and Roy Limbert, the director, in 1929, have given it a wider fame than even its waters earned for it. The festival is dedicated to George Bernard Shaw, many of whose plays have been specially written for the event, and first presented in the festival theatre.

II. DROITWICH

In a scientific treatment of the subject Droitwich would have a prominent place; in a social sketch there is little to say about it, in spite of its antiquity as a town. Droitwich has been a borough since 1215, and long before that date its salt, for centuries the symbol of hospitality, was mined and sold. To the Romans, whose coins have been found under the High Street, it was *Salinae*; to the Saxons it was *Wic*, or salt spring. When the Normans came they added the prefix *Droit* to signify that the king had taxation right. Nevertheless, as a spa Droitwich depends almost entirely on its waters, which is, perhaps, what a spa ought to depend on, though few ever did. Perhaps she suffers from being plainer than other members of the same family —after all an exceptionally handsome family.

But if Droitwich lacks some of the external attractions of the spas already visited, no other can equal it in its own field. Its naturally radio-active brine was a most generous gift from Nature, and one that has been used to good effect. The Royal Baths at Droitwich, the first curative establishment in the town, opened in 1836, and were followed by St. Andrew's Baths fifty years later. The water for these is pumped up from the Triassic formation two hundred feet below the level of the town, and appears to be inexhaustible in quantity. For density and effectiveness there is no brine in the world to equal it. Droitwich is thus pre-eminently a place for those who suffer from one of the many disabilities for which this specialised treatment is desirable. The cure is a full-time job in Droitwich.

III. CHELTENHAM

In Cheltenham, one of the most beautiful towns in England, we return to the graces and amenities of life. What Tunbridge was to the spring and Bath to the early summer of the spas, Cheltenham was to their August and September. And when the waters, curative or not, were no longer the principal interest in these so-called watering-places it adapted itself to the new life of leisure and retirement with singular charm. But more precisely, what Tunbridge was to the seventeenth century, Bath to the eighteenth, Cheltenham was to the gay and prosperous years of the Regency. Each was the most elegant creation of its period, and though Tunbridge had to be refashioned in the nineteenth century, so that it is now representative of Victorian rather than Caroline England, we are fortunate in having preserved in Bath and Cheltenham superb examples of what was done in two periods rich in craftsmanship, taste, and culture. Like Malvern, its neighbour, Cheltenham owes much to its setting, with the rolling Cotswolds at hand—hill and valley, village and farmstead of a countryside that belongs to the very heart of England and responds to no other name. Yet Cheltenham, like Bath, is not in itself conspicuously English. Let us be honest about this. These towns are among our proudest possessions; but they are not typical of our national character, either past or present. If you are English of the English you will admit that whatever the experts may say you are happier in Wells than in Bath, in Chipping Campden than in

Cheltenham. But even the English have their full-dress occasions, when, if somewhat bashfully, they are ready to admit that they like to remember how in palmier days their forbears produced such towns as Bath and Cheltenham.

Cheltenham's architecture, though it must delight the eye of every person of taste, is a specialist's subject, and I believe Mr. Bryan Little, who wrote so well on the architecture of Bath, has a key to it in preparation. All authorities agree that here we have Regency architecture at its best. 'It had the good fortune to be built,' says a report of the Georgian Group, 'with unity of purpose and at a time when contemporary taste was at a high level.... The town is one of the most attractive examples of urban development in the country.... It is particularly famous for the wealth and elegance of its architectural iron work. This is displayed in numerous balconies, verandahs, door hoods, and area railings, and in many cases this iron work forms the only decoration of the façades. Nowhere else can the characteristics of the early 19th century iron work be studied better.' But it is not in detail alone that Cheltenham is distinguished. Its principal builder, John Papworth, like John Wood of Bath, was something else besides an architect. Wood was a surveyor, Papworth a designer, and it is lay-out no less than architecture that gives Cheltenham the charm that many of us find lacking in Bath.

The waters at Cheltenham first attracted attention in 1716, and again we have the story of a well being frequented by flocks of birds. At Harrogate it was lapwings, or tewits as they are called in the North; here and at Sydenham it was pigeons, attracted, it is said, by the salt deposited by the water. Whether that is a valid reason or not must be left to the naturalists. Our present concern is with birds of a different feather. Though the enticing of these began about 1721, after the first analysis of the water by Drs. Greville and Baird, there was little result until 1738, when Captain Skillicorne, the second owner of the spa, came into possession. This gentleman cleaned the spring, built a small pump-room, and planted the first of the many avenues of limes and chestnuts for which Cheltenham was later to be renowned. But for all that Captain Skillicorne did development was slow, and this will hardly surprise us if we reflect upon the difficulties and hazards of early eighteenth-century travel in the midland counties. As an illustration of these hazards we have a letter from Mrs. Delany to Mr. Granville dated 9th August 1735, in which she says: 'We arrived here last night, I thank God, safe, after a very tedious journey, occasioned by the restiveness of two out of our six horses, four of which were hired at Warwick. We breakfasted on our way to Mickleton, and Mrs. Chapone and Sally came with us in a

55 CHELTENHAM. The Pump Room at Pittville Spa, designed by J. B. Forbes in 1825

From a contemporary lithograph by H. Lami

56 Pittville: The Pump Room from across the Lake

From an early-Victorian print

57 The Entrance to the Old Royal Wells, 1812

From a water-colour by Thomas Hulley

CHELTENHAM

Post Chaise to guide us. The road to Mickleton was most terrible, and bad enough to foil the best horses in England, but all that is over. We have got a charming lodging, and a room at your service, if you will make us a visit at Mrs. Hughes's near the Well. I begin with our glass to-morrow morning.' Five years later—in 1738—the first Cheltenham-to-London coach was advertised as making the journey in 'the short space of three days,' with the proviso, 'if God permitted.'

At this time Cheltenham was far from being the gracious and elegant town we see to-day. An advertisement in the *Gloucester Journal* of 11th August 1741 ran: 'Notice is hereby given that there will be a Cudgel Match opposite the Plough in Cheltenham on Friday the 14th inst., (beginning half an hour after two, and ending at seven the same evening). He that breaks the most heads in three bouts, and comes off clear, to receive a good hat, and a guinea in money.... N.B.—Betwixt the hours of 10 and 2, there will be a gown jigged for by the girls.'

Then, and for many years afterwards, these cudgel contests were held on a stage set up on market and fair days in front of the Bell Inn. At the same time there was bull-baiting with dogs, cock-fighting, and similar capers that would hardly have appealed to the Cheltenham of eighty or a hundred years later.

The only reliable source of information for the early years of Cheltenham's life as a spa is Captain Skillicorne's diary, in which we have a record of all the improvements made and the profits they yielded. The number of visitors is carefully entered—414 in 1740, for example, at a shilling apiece, and in 1743 'about 600 persons of great fortunes and gentility.' In round figures, attendance fluctuated during the next ten years between 450 and 650 a year, which seems few in comparison with the six or seven hundred a day attracted for a short time by the more popular London spas. Already, however, the lack of quantity—and, of course, comparison with London is hardly just— was compensated for by the presence of quality, because bad as the roads were, and rude as the accommodation was, a surprisingly large number of distinguished people did travel across the shires to drink the waters. We know that one reason for the popularity of Cheltenham and the rest of the English spas at the beginning of the nineteenth century was that the Continental spas were closed by the Napoleonic wars. This, undoubtedly, was the principal reason for their Georgian heyday. But Cheltenham had distinguished and aristocratic visitors before the wars. Handel was there in 1744 and 1749, Campbell the poet in 1774, and in the same year Mr. and Mrs. Siddons.

Most of the spas had a period of flirtation with the waters before resigning

themselves to the restriction of wedlock. The date of this wedding, if the
term may be allowed, is usually clear enough. For Cheltenham it was 1780,
and the man who tied the nuptial knot was Dr. Jenner, the discoverer of
vaccination. In the same year Simeon Moreau was appointed Master of
Ceremonies, and in the following year Cheltenham got its first published
guide—which, incidentally, has lines suggesting that the town's new status
was not appreciated by all its inhabitants:

> *Lately an ape in the shape of a beau,*
> *By the outlandish name of Monsieur M—u,*
> *Has officiously come at the balls to preside,*
> *To preserve etiquette and pay homage to pride.*

This resentment is easily understood. Cheltenham would then be similar
in character to its Cotswold neighbours of to-day, and we can imagine how
they would feel about having a Master of Ceremonies imposed on them.

But if we refer again to the Cheltenham guide of 1781 we can find evidence
of others in Cheltenham being of a different mind. These were dissatisfied
with the old ways, complaining, for example, that the street is 'encumbered
with certain old coarse buildings supported on stone pillars; these are called
the Corn Market and Butter Cross.... It is to be hoped that objects so
very unsightly will soon be removed.' Some, perhaps, would wish to
preserve these structures; but seven years later whatever resistance there was
to Cheltenham's desire for transformation was broken, for in that year
George III, his consort, and their three daughters came to drink the waters,
which meant that for better or worse Cheltenham was destined to fame.

The royal party stayed at Bayshill House, built by Captain Skillicorne
for the Earl of Fauconberg in 1781. Hitherto his Majesty had been regarded
as a healthy man, and at first his indisposition was thought to be nothing
more serious than a disordered digestion, for which his doctor, Sir George
Baker, prescribed a course of Cheltenham waters. The royal visit was M.
Moreau's opportunity, and he made the most of it. Nothing that could
contribute to the convenience and pleasure of the royal party was omitted.
A contemporary account tells us that about six-thirty p.m. on the day of
his arrival, the king, a tall, portly figure in blue coat and scarlet cape
trimmed with gold lace, high military boots, and carrying a gold-headed
cane, came down into the town, which was gaily illuminated to welcome
him, and that such was the joy of the people that even the musicians in the
theatre left their performances unfinished, and, followed by the audience,
went in procession through the town, playing and singing all the most
popular and patriotic strains they could think of. By nightfall every inn and

alehouse was packed with loyal subjects toasting his Majesty, the queen, and the princesses in round after round until the early hours of the following morning.

The king drank his first glass daily at six, followed by a second after walking with the queen for half an hour. Then about seven-thirty they returned to Bayshill for breakfast. Later in the morning the beauty spots and places of historic interest in the neighbourhood were visited, usually with the king on horseback, followed by the rest of the party in carriages. It was the king's interest in horsemanship at this time that made riding-habits fashionable in Cheltenham for generations. The ladies especially affected them, which gave Whitefoord, the wit, the opportunity of replying to the gentleman who remarked that the Cheltenham ladies had a good habit of drinking the waters early: 'Yes, sir, they have good habits in coming here, but they come in damned bad ones.'

Cheltenham has many mementos of this royal visit. In the Art Gallery there is an old print of 'King George and the Fair Quakeress,' a Cheltenham belle with whom his Majesty was fond of conversing. M. Moreau kept a diary of these historic days, and also caused a medal to be struck at his own expense, which was presented in gold and silver to their Majesties and the princesses. The king himself responded with equal appreciation. He expressed himself both delighted by the visit and greatly improved in health. On meeting a Cheltenham person on Weymouth promenade some years later he greeted him with: 'Ah, you have come from one of the finest counties of England, and good as Dorsetshire may be, it can bear no comparison with Cheltenham and the Vale of Gloucester, the finest part of my kingdom that I have beheld.' Of the many accounts of this well-remembered visit the best is Fanny Burney's, the most amusing *Peter Pindar's*, or Dr. Wolcot's, to give him his correct name.

With such royal commendation as this Cheltenham could not fail to prosper, and we have a vivid reflection of its new life of fashion in *Ruff's History and Guide* of 1803. 'The Spa (57) is opened,' it runs, 'every morning for the accommodation of visitors. The sun has no sooner begun to absorb the cool dews of the morning, and the whole sky to be animated with its warmth and influence . . . than the "busy hum" commences at the well. Between six and seven the walks begin to be filled. From seven till nine they are crowded. Here may be seen a galaxy of beauty, which overpowers even Aurora herself. Here, the sparkling eye—the bewitching mien—the elegant costume, which fascinated all beholders at the evening ball—assumes an altered character. The warm glow of the midnight dance is exchanged for the fresh tint of the morning. The brilliant robe, the necklace, the ear drop, and the head dress, are transformed into an easier, a simpler, and, perhaps, more becoming attire.'

But in appearance Cheltenham was still one with its Gloucestershire neighbours. The new town for the new life had not yet been created. When it did come into being it expressed with a felicity that was nowhere surpassed the spirit of that restrained yet assured way of life which flowered in the Regency summers and in few that have succeeded them. The seed of that flower has never been lost in Cheltenham. Consequently Cheltenham is still rooted in the living soil, and is not a dried up and artificially preserved museum piece. The problem of creating the town in which men could have a life that would be both cultured and creative was not solved in Bath, because when London went down to the country there it took the town with it, and the town has culture but not creation. In Cheltenham, knowledge and nature, humanity's lion and lamb, were able to lie down together. The solution of both the townsman's need of creation and the countryman's need of culture has been found for most men during the twentieth century in a garden. That was Cheltenham's solution. The new town was planned and built in a garden. At first such romanticism seemed strange. When the first lawns were laid and houses built round them there were few who realised that this would be the ideal pattern of the future, the logical development from the village green. When the Promenade was planned and planted in 1818 with limes and chestnuts, no-one realised that a hundred years later this would be regarded as one of the most beautiful streets in the world. Joseph Pitt, however, the builder of Pittville Pump Room, to whose vision we owe most of the Cheltenham of to-day, saw the value of what had been started, and in spite of financial loss and the ridicule of his neighbours had the courage and enterprise to complete it. His tragedy was that when the Pittville Pump Room (55, 56) was opened in 1830 the heyday of the spas was over; his triumph was that the new age of leisure was only just beginning, and it was in this that Cheltenham was to mature.

If this Regency spa was too late to do as much for the body as some of the older spas had done, it did more for the mind. All the spas have a fine educational tradition; but Cheltenham is pre-eminent. Education has been its vocation, and when the borough was incorporated in 1876 the motto 'Salubritas et Eruditio' was adopted.

IV. LEAMINGTON

Only one more major spa, Leamington, remained to be established. It had much in common with Cheltenham, and for a while they flourished together, though Leamington's spring was discovered first. Camden mentioned it in his *Britannica* of 1586; Speed referred to it; and Fuller caps all other descriptions by saying: 'at Leamington, two miles from Warwick, there issueth out, within a stride, of the womb of the earth, two twin springs, as different in tastes and operation as Jacob and Esau in disposition —the one salt, the other fresh. This the meanest countryman does plainly see by their effects; whilst it would puzzle a consultation of physicians to assign the cause thereof.' If he had been living a hundred years later he would have likened it to the Pool of Bethesda, for it was then much in vogue for the cure of people bitten by mad dogs. Yet in spite of these early references, and in spite of the fact that Dr. Guidott of Bath analysed its waters as early as 1686, its well-house was not built until 1804, and Leamington did not come into its own until the reign of Queen Victoria. It then became, according to Dr. Granville, the fashionable retreat for 'dukes and duchesses, marquesses, earls, and barons, with their coroneted partners—not to mention the Lady Augustas and Louisas....'

The spirits of the antiquary must always rise and his step quicken on entering Warwickshire. It was, of course, Shakespeare's county, and Stratford upon Avon is only ten miles from Leamington. But that is not what excites him. This, he recalls, is the county of Sir William Dugdale, that good old knight who set the pace for the great county historians of the eighteenth century, and he sends up a prayer for the repose of Sir William's soul. But if he is a good antiquary he will be somewhat abashed to notice that Sir William says the Leamington spring rises east of the church, whereas it obviously rises west of that building. These wells have always muddled men's wits. Look, for example, at the doctors. Here is Dr. Guidott in 1698 saying it is 'a spring of nitrous water,' and there is Dr. Short in his *Treatise on Mineral Waters* (1740) contradicting him and pronouncing it 'a mere brine spring.' Then seventeen years later, Dr. Rutty, with the wisdom of Solomon, restored harmony between these contentious physicians by describing it as 'a salino nitrous spring.' But let us have the facts. Leamington's development as a spa dates from the 14th of January 1784, when two local worthies, Benjamin Satchwell, who was something of a village oracle, and William Abbotts, landlord of the Black Dog inn, were standing in the roadway a short distance from the spring, discussing the refusal of the lord of the manor to accept an offer of a thousand pounds from a Dr. Holyoake for the well and a few old cottages near it. Abbotts owned a piece of land close to where they stood, and had made several attempts to discover a second spring from which he himself might profit, all of them without success. It seemed hard that they should have this potential wealth in the village and be unable to touch it. So these two neighbours were not feeling as cheerful as they might have been until, suddenly, Satchwell dropped on his knees and plunged his hand into a pool of water that had collected in the ditch nearby. He had noticed bubbles rising to the surface of the water, and with the expression on his face of one who has come upon an unexpected oasis in the desert, he drew up a draught of the water in his cupped hands and drank it. There was no doubt of it. Here was another mineral spring, and on Abbotts' land. Abbotts borrowed a cup and after tasting the water for himself agreed that it was mineral. But they were not scientists, so the water was sent for analysis to Dr. Ker, the leading physician in Northampton, who gave the spring the authority of his recommendation. That, briefly, is how Leamington became a spa.

Abbotts lost no time in building baths on the site, with a new hotel adjoining them (53). In 1790 a third spring was discovered by a Mr. Wise, and this also was given baths, which were removed later to make way for the railway. Then in 1794 a Dr. Lambe wrote the inevitable pamphlet, first published in the Memoirs of the Manchester Philosophical Society, praising the waters to such a tune that three duchesses arrived in a single season. And little wonder, for Dr. Lambe had said that the new watering-place was 'likely to cast Bath and every other Spa into the shade.' Messrs. Abbotts, Satchwell, and Wise had only to cast in their nets, for the miracle had happened again. So rapid was the growth of the new town that ten years later a foreign visitor described Leamington as 'a rich and elegant town, containing ten or twelve palace-like inns, four large bath-houses with Colonnades and gardens, several libraries, with which are connected card, billiard, concert and ballrooms (one for six hundred persons), and a host of private houses, which are almost entirely occupied by visitors and spring out of the earth like mushrooms.'[1] In 1801 its population was 315; in the twenties it rose from 2000 to 6000; in the thirties it passed the 12,000 mark; in 1891 it was close on 27,000.

The old town of Leamington was entirely on the south bank of the river. The development of the north bank was made possible by the building of the Victoria Bridge (1807-1809), and on the 8th October 1808 the first brick was laid of the new town, which with its wider parades, its gardens, and its dignified Regency squares, was to add yet one more belated achievement to the Georgian age. Hanoverian names repeat themselves, and in their symmetry, their mathematical precision, and their forms, the streets, crescents, circuses, and so forth follow the lines of Bath and Cheltenham, with, however, a greater tendency towards romanticism, shown especially in the gardens.

[1] Puckler-Muskau, quoted by M. Letts, *As the Foreigner Saw Us*, 1935.

But the seal could not be set on the new enterprise until it had received the blessing of royalty, so the great day for Leamington arrived with the visit of the Prince Regent to the recently opened Williams' Royal Hotel on Friday the 10th September 1819, after which this dignified house took the name of the Regent Hotel. At this time Leamington's season began in the middle of May and ended with Warwick September Races. The customs were the same as at other spas—early morning taking of the waters, followed by an airing on the parades; then riding and driving, tea-drinking, and all the rest of it; the whole social round culminating in a weekly ball every Thursday. In the pursuit of genteel pleasures Leamington society revolved in the prescribed circle, with no more excitement than could be caused by the arrival of a duchess, or an occasional elopement, until the recently crowned Victoria came to drink the waters in 1838 and allowed the town to assume the name of Royal Leamington Spa. It was Victoria also, now the beloved queen, who in 1875 granted the spa its charter of incorporation.

The laying out of the gardens near the river began in 1834. Several men contributed to their beauty, notably John Cullis; but by a happy gesture they were dedicated to the memory of an esteemed local doctor, and for most visitors, to think of Leamington is to see in imagination these beautiful Jephson Gardens, forming a kind of Kurgarten such as Harrogate only among the older spas could rival. If Leamington belongs to the Georgian tradition it is nevertheless a town of the Victorians. They loved it, and what better thought could we have in leaving it than Ruskin's joyous exclamation on finding that the waters had cured him: 'My health is in my own hands. I have gone back to brown potatoes and cherry pie!'

Chapter Nine

SMALLER SPAS

Arise betimes, to pump repair,
First take the waters, then the air;
Most moderate be in meat and drink,
And rarely, very rarely, think.

Bath Guide

'IT seems all waters have their ebbing and flowing: I mean in esteem,'
said Fuller, thinking of the Ebbing and Flowing Well near Skipton
in Yorkshire. They certainly had. Even Bath was thought a bore in
the eighteen-thirties, when London saw in it little more than a faded reflection of its own faded self. The same jokes were told in both places, only in
Bath they were told a little later than in London, which meant that the
bon mots of the London salons could be repeated in Bath, but not *vice versa*.
It meant also that the London beau was welcomed in Bath, but for a man
staying in London to confess himself a visitor from Bath was to commit
social suicide. Everyone longed for change. The older ladies could keep
themselves awake by talking scandal, the young of the rich and pampered
classes spent their time chasing the butterfly of novelty.

That particular generation escaped for excitement to Brighton, or to such
resorts as Ramsgate and Margate. But there was nothing new in boredom.
The idle had always been bored, and hitherto they had only had the spas.
In these they spent their money in a vain search for happiness, while usually
the happiest people around were those who had to work hard to keep the
others amused. As Messrs. Abbotts and Satchwell knew, there was no
easier way of making money than by running a successful spa, provided a
fashionable doctor could be found to recommend the water as a cure for—

> *. . . the knotted gout,*
> *The bloated dropsy and the racking stone,*
> *Rolling her eyes in anguish; lepra foul*
> *Strangling angina; ephialitic starts;*
> *Unnerv'd paralysis; with moist catarrhs;*
> *Pleuritis bending o'er its side in pain;*
> *Vertigo; murderous apoplexy . . .*

120

58 The Approach to the Hotwell House

From an aquatint of c. 1795

59 The Wells and St. Vincent's Rock

From an engraving by J. Hassell, 1793

BRISTOL HOT WELLS

60 The Hot Baths

61 The Cross Bath

Both from engravings after T. H. Shepherd

BATH IN 1829

or some other member of that grisly chorus. Consequently scores of attempts to establish new spas were made. Though the failures outnumbered the successes by at least ten to one, many places now relatively unknown as spas had their season and reaped a not inconsiderable harvest. Essex alone, a most unlikely county for spas, had twenty-four. Eight of them are mentioned by Benjamin Allen, who wrote on medicinal waters at the end of the seventeenth century—possibly because Allen himself was a Braintree doctor and not disinterested. But they continued to spring up until 1852, when the last of them, Dovercourt, was brought to public notice. Witham, which flourished in the middle of the eighteenth century, was by far the most successful. Hockley, near Southend, made a bold bid for fame, but its pump-room, which Dr. Henry Laver, the Essex antiquary, described as 'big enough for Bath,' can have had few patrons. At Mistley, near Manningtree in Essex, Richard Rigby, friend of Horace Walpole and patron of the arts in his day, established in the eighteenth century a fashionable watering-place for which Robert Adam designed the principal buildings. To-day the railway cuts through the site of Rigby's mansion; but forlorn relics of the spa remain in the towers of what was formerly the church, in the bridge, the inn, and one of the pepper-box lodges, all characteristic examples of Adam's work.

Harrison of Radwinter in his *Description of England* refers to King's Newman, near Coventry, which was the subject of a short monograph (1587) by Dr. Walter Bayley, one of the queen's physicians, who says that though the waters *might* be used in leap years he himself would not advise it! Wellingborough in Northamptonshire was visited for its waters by Queen Henrietta Maria, and in 1624 by the Duke of Buckingham along with his wife and mother. At this time it was so popular that the Lord Chamberlain thought of building a house nearby. Hail Weston, near St. Neots, had two springs that were in high repute at the time, as we know from Drayton's *Polyolbion*, where Wellingborough also is mentioned. Astrop in Northamptonshire was another popular Restoration spa in this part of the country. Indeed, by 1712, according to John Morton, Northamptonshire had thirty-eight mineral springs, which was obviously far more than most counties; but at a modest estimate we may say that several of the larger counties had between ten and twenty apiece, and that few were completely barren. Oxfordshire had about fifteen; Leigh, in his *Natural History of Lancashire, Cheshire, and the Peak of Derbyshire* (1700) mentions twenty; Plot, in the *Natural History of Staffordshire* (1686), has nineteen, with the interesting note that the people in that county still adorned their wells—which were, of course, old holy wells—'at some certain times of the year, with green boughs and flowers, in grateful memory of the good they have formerly done.' The rate of increase appears to have been as great in the first thirty or forty years of the eighteenth century as it was in the last thirty of the seventeenth; but with the important difference that whereas most of the springs brought to public notice in the earlier period were pre-Reformation holy wells that had been neglected—with a few exceptions—for two or three generations, those in the later period were secular. Some idea of the number of English spas in the middle of the eighteenth century can be gained from a glance at Thomas Short's *History of Mineral Waters*, which deals only with the Midlands, the North of England, and one or two Scottish spas. Bath, Tunbridge Wells, and Epsom are not described. Yet in the first volume of this work, published in 1734, a hundred and thirty-four 'spaws' are noticed, and in the second volume, published in 1740, we have a further ninety-four, 'besides several others of less note.' It should, however, be understood that by 'spaw' Dr. Short means a mineral spring, and some parishes therefore have several. It is difficult to reconcile the intrinsic value of their water with the popular esteem of some of Dr. Short's wateringplaces. For example, far more fame than it ever enjoyed might have been expected for Orston Spa on the Duke of Kingston's estate, about ten miles from Nottingham, if the doctor was any judge. 'This water,' he says, 'is replete with a mineral spirit to a prodigy. When fresh poured out into a glass, it sparkles and flies and makes the drinker's head very giddy.'

The eastern counties, apart from Yorkshire, were not rich in spas. Norfolk had one at Thetford, Suffolk one at Ipswich and another at Bungay. Lincolnshire—curiously enough—had no spa at the beginning of the eighteenth century. Then Stainfield, about ten miles from Stamford, found its Æsculapius in Dr. Edward Greethead of Lincoln, and the people from the neighbourhood visited it in such numbers that in 1720 a well house was built for their convenience. Another spa was discovered at Cawthorpe, about two miles away, and gradually Lincolnshire got its quota, though it was not until 1811 that its one spring to achieve a national reputation was discovered. This, of course, gave rise to Woodhall Spa, now a residential health resort with a population of about fifteen hundred. The Woodhall spring was struck at a depth of 520 feet when a Mr. John Parkinson sank a shaft there in the hope of finding coal. It proved to be exceptionally rich in iodine and bromine; but attracted much less attention than it deserved until the spa estate was bought by a syndicate in 1886, when a bath-house was provided and a new town, sheltered by woodlands and sweetened by the scent of pines, was built on this breezy Lincolnshire heath.

Another spring found while searching for coal was the one at Ashby-dela-Zouch in Leicestershire, struck at a depth of 700 feet in 1805, which proved to be rich in sodium chloride.

Several of the Yorkshire springs were probably struck in the same way, though Yorkshire has always been a great county for spas. The waters of Thirsk were said to sparkle like champagne. The Harrogate and Scarborough districts had whole constellations of lesser lights. Among the better-known Yorkshire spas were Malton, with mineral springs similar to those at Scarborough, Whitby, Middleton near Pickering, Beverley, Tadcaster, Horley Green and Slaithwaite near Halifax, Atwith near Pontefract, Barnsley, Leeds, Wakefield, Addingham, Skipton, Broughton, Wigglesworth, and Ilkley; but with the exceptions of Ilkley and Malton none of them had any kind of social life to distinguish them from the rest of their prolific kind. Ilkley's advantages are obvious. Like Malvern, which in several ways it resembles, its waters are remarkable for their purity, not their mineral content, and like Malvern again it owes much to its breezy moorland setting.

Many of the Northern spas were sulphur springs, and not very pleasant either to smell or taste. A Doncaster physician, Dr. Edward Chorley, on passing through Askerne, with its strong sulphuretted effluvia, composed the rhyme:

> The devil when passing through Askeron
> Was asked what he thought thereon;
> Quoth Satan, 'Judging from the stink,
> I can't be far from home, I think.'

Of the spas farther north, Shap, a favourite with Sir Joseph Simpson, was the most successful. Others were Croft, Dinsdale (38), Guisborough, Shotley Bridge, and Gilsland (39). Clitheroe, an old town of character in the Ribble Valley, with some of the most beautiful dale and moorland scenery in the North of England at hand, might well have become a spa if a local apothecary named Sutcliffe, who discovered its sulphur spring, built a bath-house, and laid out gardens, had not died before completing his plan.

In the West, Gloucester had a small Regency spa, some relics of which may still be seen. But it was Bath that had the most interesting group of smaller springs. About four miles outside the city we find the well of St. Catharine, the patroness of philosophical studies, who at eighteen was condemned to be broken on a wheel for defending her Christian faith. Other holy wells near Bath were St. Mary's Well, Charlecombe; St. Anthony's Well, Bathford; and St. Alphage's Well, Lansdown, which is probably the only well in England dedicated to this particular saint. Nearby, at Chapel Farm, was a hospice used by pilgrims travelling to Glastonbury, which had a famous holy well, while in Bath itself there was St. Winifred's Well on Sion Hill, Lansdown, one of the wells used by ladies who wished to become mothers.

After Bath, the most important spa in this region, and by far the most important of the spas not yet named, was Clifton, now a suburb of Bristol. John Leland has a description of St. Anne's Well, near the city, which was

served by priests from the Augustinian abbey at Keynsham. He says 'A 2 miles above Bristow was a Commune Trajectus by bote, wher was a Chapelle of S. Anne, on the same side of Avon that Bath stondith on, and heere was great Pilgrimage to S. Anne.' Candles were kept burning before the saint's image by local craft guilds, and her chapel was hung with the grateful offerings of seamen who relied on her protection while following their hazardous calling. Henry VII visited this shrine of St. Anne-in-the-Wood, as it was popularly called, after dining in state with the Mayor, Sheriffs, and Bailiffs on a famous occasion.

But it was the Hotwells (58) that brought society to Clifton in such force that during the season London tradesmen opened shops there, as they did at Tunbridge Wells and Scarborough. The original spring was known at least

62 Bristol Hot Wells in the Seventeenth Century

as early as 1632. In 1695 the Bristol merchants granted a lease, with provisions for the protection of the spring and the erection of a pump. The second spring, known as the New Hotwell, was first noticed in 1702. During the eighteenth century a fashionable resort was built round them, with long-room and assembly-room close to the river and commanding fine views of the gorge. There were public breakfasts, country dances, a library, and all the amenities to be expected at a well-appointed spa. An M.C.

presided over the entertainments, keeping the company to rules based on those drawn up by Beau Nash for Bath and Tunbridge Wells.

Clifton Hotwells are mentioned by Fanny Burney in *Evelina,* and they had an unexpected visitor in John Wesley, who, incidentally, had more to do with the spas than we might think. Bath, Bristol, and Tunbridge Wells had vigorous Nonconformist communities. Wesley's visit, on the advice of his doctor, was in 1754, when consumption was suspected. After taking a course of the waters he recovered in a remarkable manner, and afterwards proved a most valuable publicity agent. Matthew Bramble in *Humphry Clinker* brings his usual sardonic humour to bear on the inconveniences of Clifton life. Lydia Melford, on the other hand, gives an ecstatic account of it in a letter to Miss Letty Willis at Gloucester—her 'dear Letty': 'We set out for Bath to-morrow,' she writes, and we can see the wringlets framing her pensive face as she takes up her quill. . . . 'We leave for Bath to-morrow, and I am almost sorry for it; as I begin to be in love with solitude, and this is a charming romantic place. The air is so pure; the Downs so agreeable; the furze in full blossom; the ground enamelled with daisies, and primroses, and cowslips; all the trees bursting into leaves, and the hedges already clothed with their vernal livery; the mountains covered with flocks of sheep, and tender bleating wanton lambkins playing, frisking and skipping from side to side . . . and all night long sweet Philomel pours forth her ravishing delightful song. Then, for variety, we go down to the *nymph of Bristol spring,* where the company is assembled before dinner; so good natured, so free, so easy; and there we drink the water so clear, so pure, so mild, so charmingly maukish.'

This gay, romantic, sentimental life came to an end about 1870, when the Docks Committee removed Hotwells Point, and in doing so pulled down both the assembly-room and the pump-room, built in 1722, from the windows of which Lydia Melford had gazed in bemused excitement at what she called the 'enchanting variety of moving pictures.' It was part of the committee's scheme to improve river navigation. Previously the Merchant Venturers, who retain an interest in the land, had controlled the site, and it was one of the conditions between them and the Docks Committee that the spring should again be made accessible by means of a grotto, hollowed out of the rock. This was done, and, according to an interesting account of the Clifton Hotwells in the Bristol Evening Post of the 27th January 1948, a census showed that approximately three hundred and fifty visitors a day took the waters up to 1912-13, when the well had to be closed because river water was seeping through and polluting it. In the hope of striking the spring farther back two borings were made, but they proved abortive.

Another hot spring, the old Zion Spring, is still to be found on the property of the Grand Spa Hotel; but this also was rendered impure by rock fissure. There is still considerable local interest in the Clifton Hotwells, and it is quite possible that their medicinal properties will again be made available.

Although, as we have seen, the heyday of the spas was over by 1830, in 1841 we have Dr. Granville in his three-volume work on *The spas of England* describing in a most tedious manner at least sixty-seven of them. Some, even then, were of recent discovery. And because the easy-money days were over, the doctors, in crying their virtues, were more prone than ever to echo the language of that lively broadsheet of 1684,[1] *An Exclamation from Tunbridge and Epsom Against the Newfound Wells at Islington*: 'Interlopers are abroad, and we must cry out as the Quack Doctors doe—*Beware of Counterfeits, for they swarm*; could not folks be content to invent new *Fashions* and new *Oaths*, new *Religions*, and new Models of Government, but the Divil must put them upon finding out *new Wells*, and new *Physical Waters*, when there were old ones enough of all Conscience, to have scour'd their *Gutts*, and purged their *Purses* and make work for the *Doctors*.' There was no fear that the doctors might lose their influence at the spas; but they were no longer able to make any old well serve their purpose with the superstitious and gullible. Science was to show that there was, in fact, more virtue in these medicinal waters than anyone had understood. Doctors of unquestionable integrity and of the highest skill were later to use them with apparently miraculous effect; but when that day came the number of spas was reduced from hundreds to a dozen or so.

[1] Quoted by Reginald Lennard, *Englishmen at Rest and Play*, Clarendon Press, 1931, pp. 36-7.

Chapter Ten

A FLURRY OF PHYSICIANS

The first physicians by debauch were made,
Excess began, and sloth sustained the trade. . .
The wise for cure on exercise depend,
God never made his work for man to mend.

Dryden

IN scanning the history of the spas it would be difficult to decide which
did more for the other, the doctor for the spa, or the spa for the doctor.
As we have seen, their fortunes rose and fell together, and both
flourished far more on wine than ever they did on water. Indeed, the
redoubtable Sir Theodore Mayerne (64), physician to the queens of James I
and Charles I, a pioneer for treatment at the spas, recommended a monthly
bout at trencher and bottle as a stimulant to the system. He lived to be
eighty-two and remained a *bon vivant* to the end. Sad to relate, however, he
died from an overdose of his own—or the vintner's—medicine. But he
blamed the fatal indisposition on the badness of the wine. 'Good wine,'
he had often said, 'is slow poison. I have drunk it all my lifetime, and it
has not killed me yet; but bad wine is sudden death.'

Mayerne, incidentally, wrote the best cookery book of his day, and perhaps his most renowned recipe was what he called 'A City of London Pie.'
Here it is:

'Take eight marrow bones, eighteen sparrows, one pound of potatoes, a
quarter of a pound of eringoes, two ounces of lettuce stalks, forty chestnuts,
half a pound of dates, a peck of oysters, a quarter of a pound of preserved
citron, three artichokes, twelve eggs, two sliced lemons, a handful of pickled
barberries, a quarter of an ounce of whole pepper, half an ounce of sliced
nutmeg, half an ounce of whole cinnamon, a quarter of an ounce of whole
cloves, half an ounce of mace, and a quarter of a pound of currants. Liquor
when it is baked with white wine, butter, and sugar.'

After such dishes as that, who could doubt the necessity of a course of
purgative waters?

It is not at all improbable, in spite of his advanced age, that the intervention of Bacchus saved the doctor from one of his own less palatable

prescriptions. Admirable as he was in the kitchen, he was an ogre in the dispensary. Judging by his recorded remedies, he would have been more at home with a witch's cauldron than with an apothecary's gallipot. Pulverised human bones seems to have been one of his favourite ingredients. For his famous gout-powder he used 'raspings of a human-skull unburied.' While for his 'Balsam of Bats,' which he prescribed for cases of hypochondria, he required adders, bats, sucking-whelps, earth-worms, hog's grease, the marrow of a stag, and the thigh bone of an ox.

Quacks have flourished in every age, but nowhere more profitably than at the spas. We need not go far for the reason. A notorious quack of the eighteenth century named Rock was sitting one day in a coffee-house on Ludgate Hill when a gentleman present, not knowing who heard him, expressed surprise that a physician he esteemed highly had only a small practice while that mountebank Rock, whom every man of sense knew to be a fraud, was able to make a fortune. Rock at once made himself known, and suggested that if the speaker had been as sensible as he pretended to be he would not have been surprised.

'How many wise men, think you,' he asked, 'are there in the multitude that pass along this street?'

'About one in twenty,' replied the other.

'Well, then,' said Rock, 'the nineteen come to me when they are sick, and the physician is welcome to the twentieth.'

Such men as Mayerne were not quacks; but they took more pains over the nineteen than they did over the twentieth!

The physicians of Charles II's reign, when the English spas emerged, had far more faith in potations than in powders. They tippled gloriously. Among the most renowned of the royal physicians-in-ordinary were Tobias Whitaker, a Norfolk man, and John Archer, who came from Dublin. Neither can ever have offended their indulgent master by such advice as that given by Dr. Abernethy to the young man who, when he asked for a cure, was told to live on sixpence a day and earn it. Whether these sixpences could have supported the patients or not, they could certainly not have supported the spa doctors! Whitaker, like Mayerne, wrote on wine as well as water, and much more intelligibly on the former than on the latter. His claims for the virtues of the grape could hardly have been bettered, as the title of his treatise indicates: 'The Tree of Humane Life, or the Bloud of the Grape. Proving the possibilitie of maintaining humane life from infancy to extreame old age without any sicknesse by the use of Wine.'

While Whitaker recommended drinking, Archer recommended smoking. Well might this ingenious pair have recited the lines by Hilaire Belloc:

63 BATH: Dr. Oliver and Mr. Peirce examining patients, 1742

From the painting by William Hoare

64 Sir Theodore Mayerne, 1573–1655

From the portrait, studio of Rubens

Of old when folk lay sick and sorely tried
The doctors gave them physic, and they died.
But here's a happier age: for now we know
Both how to make men sick and keep them so.

Archer actually sold tobacco, which he claimed to be of a superior brand, and consequently he charged a much higher price for it. 'Tobacco smoke,' he said, 'purifies the air from infectious malignancy by its fragrancy, sweetens the breath, strengthens the brain and memory, and revives the sight to admiration.' These desirable ends were guaranteed to those who smoked his own mixture, which was to be taken like any other tobacco, and at any time of day; 'its virtues,' he promised, 'may be perceived by taking one pipe, after which you will spit more, and your mouth will be dryer than after common tobacco.'

In his *Every Man his Own Doctor*, Archer offers wonderful cures by remedies known only to himself, which he is willing to sell to credulous readers, evidently disregarding the fact that if the cures had to be bought from him the reader would hardly be his own doctor. One of his secret concoctions guarantees a man immunity from the effects of debauchery. Others are of similarly dubious character, and before sending a copy of *Every Man his Own Doctor* to a subscriber Archer had these words written on the fly-leaf: 'The author is to be spoke with at his chamber in a sadler's house over against the mewes gate next the Black Horse nigh Charing Cross; his howers there are from eleven to five in the evening, at other times at his house in Knightsbridge.'

Smollett, who had an idea of practising in Bath himself, was unsparing in his exposures of these spa physicians, many of whom divided their time between London and the fashionable resorts. He tells us that most of them kept in touch with correspondents in London—snoopers, who made their living by supplying information about the character, habits, and means of visitors to the baths, thus enabling the doctors to know where to bestow and where to withhold their compliments and felicitations. Smollett got much of his information for the work from Anstey's *The New Bath Guide*, where we meet several doctors of the riper sort. There is an hilarious description of Mr. Simkin Blunderhead's experiences at the hands of the doctors of Bath, one of whom diagnoses the illness of Tabitha Runt as chlorosis, aggravated

By swallowing stuff she had read in the papers;
And often I've marvell'd she spent so much money
In Water-dock essence, and Balsam of honey.

There were some, of course, of a different kidney; though Dr. Edward Jorden (1569-1632), described by Dr. Guidott, the well-known medical historian of Bath (who, as we have just seen, first analysed the Leamington water), as 'a learned, candid, and sober physician,' wrote in the preface to his *Discourse of Natural Bathes and Mineral Waters* (1631): 'Empiricks and Juggling Medicasters do so much abound, that 'tis almost as hard a matter now to meet with a regular and accomplished physician as it was in former times for Diogenes to meet with an honest man.' Jorden, incidentally, would deserve to be remembered if only for the enlightenment he showed in exposing an alleged case of witchcraft, which he examined at the invitation of James I, cleverly extracting a confession of fraud and reducing the case to its inherent absurdity. But he was worthy of honour on many counts. A man of great personal distinction, dignified, handsome, of charming address, and simple, unaffected goodness of life, there seems to have been hardly a virtue that he did not possess.

What Jorden was to the Bath of the first half of the seventeenth century, Dr. Robert Peirce (d. 1697) was to that of the second half. And as he flourished at the time of the city's rise to fortune his influence was immense. By solid worth he built up the largest practice of his day, and remained the leading doctor in the spa for fifty years, in spite of continuous attempts by scores of unscrupulous rivals to supplant him, particularly in the favour of Charles II and Queen Catharine of Braganza. His most considerable rival was Dr. Guidott himself, whose family may have come from Italy. At all events, Italian ancestry was the usual explanation of Guidott's ardour, quickness of parts, and, to give him credit for virtues he undoubtedly possessed, his culture and gifts as a man of letters. Guidott's learning was immense. If only he could have controlled his pen, he would have held in the society of his day the position to which his merits entitled him; but as he attacked practically all his fellow doctors in one or other of his writings it is not surprising that they had little use for him.

One of the spa physicians with whom Dr. Guidott engaged in acrimonious controversy was a Lancashire man—probably born at Preston—named Edward Baynard, who left an account of the visit to Bath of Alexander Selkirk, the original of Robinson Crusoe. Indeed Baynard and Defoe must have met Selkirk almost together, which would be at the time Defoe was staying in Bath while collecting material for his *Tour through the Island of Great Britain*. Selkirk is described by Baynard as 'a Scotchman, who from a leaky ship was, upon his own request, set on shore on an island in the South Sea call'd Juan Fernandes, about the latitude of 33 degrees, where he liv'd alone, and eat nothing but goat's flesh and drank water, having neither bread nor salt, as he told me himself at the Bath, where I met him; and that he was three times as strong, by exercise and such a diet, as ever he was in his life: But, when taken up by the two ships, the Duke and Duchess, set out from Bristol for the South Sea, that eating the ship-fare with the other seamen, and drinking beer, and other fermented liquors, his strength by degrees began to leave him, like cutting off Samson's hair, crinit'm (to make a word) or lock by lock; so that in one month's time he had not more strength than another man.'

Another visitor to Bath described by Dr. Baynard was William Penn, the founder of Pennsylvania, with whom he discussed the Indians' method of curing themselves of fevers by inducing a sweat and then bouncing into cold water.

But the Bath doctor whose name lives in the popular mind is Dr. Oliver, and it lives, ironically, in the name of a biscuit! William Oliver, M.D., F.R.S. (63), was the illegitimate son of another Dr. Oliver, an able physician and a generous-hearted man, if somewhat eccentric. The second Dr. Oliver was the first physician officially appointed to the Water Hospital. He was the obvious choice, for he had himself recommended the erection of a cold bath in the city to supplement the hot baths for which it was always best known. Oliver's recommendation of cold bathing is particularly interesting if we remember when it was made, because it is one more instance of the widespread advocacy of cold bathing just then, influenced in particular by Sir John Floyer of Lichfield. We might remark also that Baynard's interest in Penn's account of the Indian practice is yet another illustration of the growing conviction that the stimulating effects of cold water might be more beneficial in many cases than the hitherto applauded hot baths.

Oliver, of course, ranks with Nash, Allen, and the two Woods as one of the five founders of Bath. What Allen and the Woods did for its building, Nash for its social life, Oliver did for its waters. Without his part the others could never have established a spa, whatever else the city might have become. Like Allen, Oliver was a Cornishman, and it was undoubtedly due to the other's friendship that he rose so quickly to prominence, though his continued success was no less certainly the result of his own merits both as a man and as a doctor. As R. A. L. Smith has it in his book on *Bath*, 'In his person and life's work William Oliver represents all that was best in the gay and frivolous age of Beau Nash.'

No more generous-hearted doctor than William Oliver ever lived in Bath, or any other spa. Though he became eminent at the time when the city was making its great and successful bid for the patronage of the wealthy, he never forgot his duty as a doctor to heal the poor as well as the rich, and it was this concern for those who could not afford to pay for treatment that moved him to found the Bath General Hospital, afterwards to be called the Royal Mineral Water Hospital. The recipe used in making his famous biscuit he bequeathed to his coachman, Atkins, who opened a shop in Green Street and made a fortune out of it.

There were few doctors of the early eighteenth century with Dr. Oliver's fine sense of duty. His professional status had risen with remarkable rapidity since the Restoration, when he acquired his coach. By the end of the century this had become one of the two or three quite indispensable requisites of the fashionable town practitioner. Previously he had gone his rounds on horse-back, though usually riding side-saddle, seated on a foot-cloth, in a comfortable pillion fitted with arms and back supports, while a servant with a leading rein managed the horse.

We may say that by the time Queen Anne came to the throne every doctor in the southern spas had his carriage and four, and the very wealthy might have six horses. The doctor of Anne's reign was an imposing figure, usually dressed in black—velvet preferred—who wore a full-bottomed wig, and, in order to keep his hands delicate and supple for feeling the pulses of his lady patients, always carried a large fur muff in winter. Sir Edward Greaves, physician-in-ordinary to the king, often practising in Bath, and taking the lead among his brethren not more by his rank and wealth than by his personal skill, was one such dandy, though in wealth he seems to have been surpassed by Samuel Baue, a native of Cologne, renowned for two things besides medical proficiency—his knowledge of languages and his fashionable costume. His patients had the pleasure of seeing him ' day by day in purple velvet, and the finest linen much bedecked with lace.' In Harrogate and Buxton, however, the doctors still went their rounds on horseback.

But in addition to these interesting items of dress there was the cane. The cane was the doctor's professional insignia. He would never dream of paying a professional call without it. It was a highly polished staff, gold- or silver-headed, and as a rule this expensive knob could be removed to allow the fumes from a vinaigrette, neatly fitted into a well in the stick, to rise and protect the doctor's delicate nostrils from the noxious exhalations of the sick. Thus:

Physic of old her entry made
Beneath th'immense full-bottomed shade;
While the gilt cane, with solemn pride,
To each sagacious nose applied,
Seem'd but a necessary prop
To bear the weight of wig at top.

Many of the spa doctors were, in fact, medicine-men in the magical sense of the term, with spells and charms and fetishes. There was a Dr. Anodyne, who prescribed the wearing of certain necklaces of his own invention to help children through their teething troubles. But what might we not expect of this ingenious physician for he held the touching belief that woodcocks and cuckoos made annual journeys to the moon!

By the middle of the eighteenth century most of these popular physicians were as far removed from the sage and godly doctors—such as Drs. Jones and Deane—of the late sixteenth and early seventeenth centuries as they were from the sane and competent practitioners of to-day. Dear old Dr. Turner, Dean of Wells and chief physician to Edward VI, one of the first to write on the spas, gave counsel that might well be commended still. Writing in the middle of the sixteenth century, his advice was: 'Then after you have confessed yourself before Almighty God, and to such as you have offended, in the name of God take counsel with some learned physician who is sent of God, and not of some self-made idol, who is sent of himself. If he use all lawful means to heal you, yet you feel yourself no better, then shall it be high time to go to the baths as to the sheet-anchor. But before going to the baths, in any wise you must go to some learned physician, that by his advice you may go unto such baths, as he shall think most mete for your disease. . . . When you go homeward, make but small journeys and beware of surfeiting and of cold, and when you are at home use measureable exercise daily, and honest mirth and pastime with honest company, and beware of surfeiting in any wise, and of anger, and of too much study or carefulness.' Drs. Jones and Deane, as we saw at Buxton and Harrogate, wrote in similar strain.

Such counsels of moderation as we find at the Northern spas would hardly have been acceptable to the dandies of Bath and Tunbridge Wells—certainly not to John Hill (1716?-1775), who might be seen driving about in a fine carriage one month and the next might be languishing in a debtor's prison. A glance at a list of Hill's works in the British Museum catalogue will show that whatever else he may have been he was never idle. After serving his apprenticeship, this son of a Lincolnshire parson set up as an apothecary in St. Martin's Lane; but early in his career he turned his attention to botany, and after travelling all over England collecting plants he wrote his first botanical work. Unfortunately, he failed to get enough subscribers and had to forego publication. He next tried to supplement the small income he derived from his neglected business by playing with considerable feeling the part of the half-starved apothecary in *Romeo and Juliet*. When this failed to bring him fame he turned again to writing, and showed that he had undoubtedly a gift for popularising knowledge, however superficial his learning might be. So successful did he become as a writer that he was said at one time to be making £1,500 a year by his pen. When the king asked Dr. Johnson what he thought of Hill, the doctor replied: 'He was an ingenious man, but had no veracity.' No doubt that was true. With the money he made as a writer, he bought a coach and set up as a fashionable family doctor. This turned out to be a most profitable enterprise, because he was able to pick up all the gossip of the day from his patients, and this he turned to good account in his books.

With financial success Hill's ambition rose, and he even presumed to publish a guinea quarto entitled *God and Nature*. But like many another fluent writer he allowed his pen to outrun both his knowledge and his honour, with the result that his public lost confidence in him, and he was obliged to return for a while to his gallipots. But again his first love—Botany—called him. He bought a house and garden in Bayswater, the site now occupied by Lancaster Gate, and there grew plants from which he distilled essences that became the most popular remedies of the day. Everyone in fashionable London tried his 'essence of water-dock,' 'tincture of valerian,' 'tincture of bardana,' and 'pectoral balsam of honey,' although Garrick dismissed him with the epigram:

> For physic and farces his equal there scarce is;
> His farces are physic, his physic a farce is.

On the death of his first wife, the daughter of a domestic servant, Hill married a sister of Lord Ranelagh, and thus gained for himself the patronage of the aristocracy, which brought him such commissions as that from Lord Petre to lay out his gardens at Thorndon in Essex. Encouraged by social success, his literary ambition again mounted, this time on wings so strong that he produced his monumental work, *The Vegetable System*—twenty-four folio volumes embellished with sixteen hundred engravings of twenty-six thousand plants, all of which were drawn from nature. For this he received a Swedish order of knighthood and promptly assumed the title of Sir John.

The last embarrassment of this ill-starred child of fortune was an attack of gout, the very disease that his 'tincture of bardana' had been guaranteed to cure. He died on the 21st November 1775, and his enemies celebrated the event with the lines:

> 'Poor Doctor Hill is dead! Good lack!'
> 'Of what disorder?' 'An attack
> Of gout.' 'Indeed! I thought that he

Had found a wondrous remedy.'
'Why, so he had, and when he tried,
He found it true—the doctor died!'

Doctors were always a favourite topic of gossip at the spas, particularly at Bath, though in truth some of them could hardly have failed to provide entertainment anywhere. John Aubrey's brother Tom, it may be recalled, was attended by 'no very learned physician,' but by 'old drunken Jack Chapman, some tyme apothecary at Bath.' Dr. Johnson praised Dr. Cheyne, who lived on friendly terms with many of the most eminent men of his day, including Richardson, the novelist. At one time Cheyne was so prodigiously fat that he weighed thirty-two stone, which he reduced to slimness by becoming a vegetarian. Another Bath physician, Dr. Flemyng, who weighed twenty stone, eleven pounds, reduced himself to similar elegant proportions by swallowing a quarter of an ounce of common Castile soap every night. There seem to have been several notoriously fat men in Somerset at this time. There was a Mr. Tantley, whom Cheyne met at dinner one day:

'Tantley,' said the doctor, after a momentary silence, 'what are you thinking about?'

'I was thinking,' replied Tantley, 'how it will be possible to get either you or me into the grave after we die.'

'Six or eight stout fellows will do the business for me, but you must be taken at twice,' retorted Cheyne.

Perhaps the only man in Bath who could take a rise out of Dr. Cheyne was Beau Nash, whom he attended. The story is told of them that after the doctor had prescribed a certain medicine for the beau he asked whether the direction had been followed.

'No, i'faith, doctor, I haven't followed it,' replied Nash, ''pon honour, if I had I should have broken my neck, for I threw it out of my bed-room window.'

One of the most eccentric among the fashionable doctors of the spas in their heyday was Dr. John Radcliffe, whose name is perpetuated in the Radcliffe Library at Oxford. Like many another so-called eccentric, Radcliffe (66) had his moments of illumination, and it was in one of these that he prescribed for the overstudious Alexander Pope, then a youth of sixteen, fresh air and exercise instead of the expensive remedies advocated by most of his contemporaries. He was fifty-two when he brought the stimulus of his bracing personality to counter the effects of the hot air of Bath. Indeed, much of his alleged eccentricity seems to have amounted to little more than speaking the truth and administering common sense at unseasonable times.

The most tactless instance of this was when he was summoned to attend
Queen Anne, said to be languishing after the death of her sister—who,
incidentally, had hated her, and for whom she had no reason to pine.
Perhaps Dr. Radcliffe knew how little love there had been between the
sisters, and thought it arrant nonsense to pretend that the Queen was sor-
rowing at Mary's death. Anyhow, he was sitting in his favourite tavern
with a bottle of Tokay before him when the messenger arrived, and he said
at once that he was not going to be disturbed for any woman, not even for
the queen, adding that there was nothing wrong with her Majesty. She was
as well as anyone else if she would only think so. When this reply was
reported to Anne, she flew into a rage and dismissed him from the royal
service.

The last of the old silk-coated doctors was Henry Revell Reynolds, one
of George III's physicians, who continued to carry his gold-headed cane to
the end of his life, and to wear his well-powdered wig, silk coat and breeches,
his lace ruffles and his buckled shoes.

65 'Total Immersion'

66 Dr. John Radcliffe, 1650–1714

From the portrait by John Closterman

67 Service at the Yew Tree Well

68 The Coffin Well

TISSINGTON WELL-DRESSING, ABOUT 1900

Chapter Eleven

FROM HOLY WELLS TO
WATERING-PLACES

I

Lo here the chief solace against all tribulation
To all that be sick, bodily or ghostly,
Calling to Our Lady devoutly.

Old Ballad

II

They eat, and drink, and scheme, and plod—
They go to Church on Sunday;
And many are afraid of God—
And more of Mrs. Grundy.

IN the course of this brief sketch of English spa life it will have become
clear that there are two lines of development, the scientific and the
social. The one is seen best at Bath, Buxton, Harrogate, and Droitwich; the other at Tunbridge Wells, Bath (the chief point of intersection),
Malvern, Cheltenham, and Leamington. It will also have become clear that
behind both the scientific and the social there is either a religious or a
superstitious element. Most of the spas had been holy wells. It might be
thought that this aspect of the subject should have been examined more
carefully earlier. But if it had been, we might have been drawn down count-
less byways and never have reached Cheltenham and Leamington at all. To
begin with the holy wells would be like beginning a study of the towns of
a given county with an examination of their villages, which admittedly may
be towns in embryo. But now that we have looked at the spas themselves we
may sit back and reflect on their growth from holy wells to inland pleasure
resorts. Before doing so, however, we must remember that even the holy
wells were not always Christian. The oldest were pagan in origin. 'Where
a spring rises or a river flows,' declared Seneca, 'there ought we to build
altars and offer sacrifices.'

Nothing, surely, could be more natural or inevitable than this worship
of springs, particularly in the drier eastern countries. Consequently, no

custom could be harder to abolish for the early Christian missionaries. The altar could be destroyed, the image that stood on it broken; but the water continued to flow from the rock, filling the well and restoring life. Sir Laurence Gomme in *Etymology in Folklore* says that well-worship prevailed in every part of England—indeed it prevailed in every part of the three kingdoms. And to-day something not unlike it is still to be found, for people who believe in neither god nor devil will tell you strange tales about the supernatural powers of an old well, and these ancient beliefs are worth glancing at, because they have so much in common with apparently meaningless customs practised at the spas.

Both the Saxon king Edgar[1] and the Danish Canute (1018) issued edicts prohibiting the worshipping of wells and fountains; but in the canons of Anselm (1102) we find a compromise in the order that no-one should attribute sanctity to a fountain 'without the bishop's authority.' Gradually the Christian was substituted for the pagan during the centuries that followed, though much of the old superstition persisted. Some of the early Christian writers saw this as an evil for which the priests of the old faith were answerable.

In the West and North of England, where folk memory is less disturbed than it is in the Home Counties, we find legends and country rhymes that reflect this pagan belief in the supernatural power, often sinister, of wells. Many of them, like rivers, are said to claim human victims:

> *River of Dart, river of Dart!*
> *Every year thou claimst a heart.*

In the North, both wells and rivers are inhabited by local deities. The Tees has Peg Powler. Jenny Greenteeth is to be reckoned with in the Lancashire streams. Near the Ribble at Clitheroe, in the grounds of Waddow Hall, is a well inhabited by Peg O'Nell, who was long blamed by the folk of the neighbourhood for whatever went wrong in their lives. It is said that every seven years she claims a victim, and it was long the custom to drown a bird or animal in the river on Peg's night to appease her. Such a custom might appear strange to-day; a generation ago, however, there were still many who could pray with the old Scots peasant:

'O Lord, Thou knowest that well would it be for me this day an' I had stoopit my knees and my heart before Thee in spirit and in truth as often as I have stoopit them after this well. *But we maun keep the customs of our Fathers.*'

These local deities may not always be old as age goes among the gods;

[1] 16th Canon (A.D. 963).

but Thor's Well at Burnsall in the Craven district of Yorkshire, now called St. Helen's Well, is probably pre-Christian, while in Wanswell, near Berkeley Castle in Gloucestershire, we have a possible survival of a pagan well that has never been christened. It is said by some Gloucestershire antiquaries to take its name from Woden, popularly called Wan, god of the well-worshipping Saxons, which may explain why so many holy wells are dedicated to St. Anne. The change from Wan to Anne would be the easiest for the missionaries to impose on the superstitious pagans.

To understand the place of the well in pagan village life we have to remember that besides being the home of the god, who had, the people thought, to be propitiated with sacrifices or the water supply would be cut off, it was the social centre of the village. Everyone met at the well. So when the Christian missionaries came into a district the well was the most suitable place for them to preach from, particularly as it could afterwards be used for baptising converts. It was also the key to the confidence of the fear-ridden folk who used it. Once they saw that their spring ran and sparkled under the new god as bountifully as it had done under the old they were no longer unwilling to be converted. In the Proceedings of the Somerset Archaeological Society, vol. xxxix, the Rev. F. W. Weaver suggests that St. Aldhelm, the seventh-century bishop of Sherborne whose well at Doulting is one of the best-known holy wells of Somerset, probably preached at St. Barbara's Well, Cucklington, and baptised in its water. Such a well would almost certainly be the object of pagan worship before St. Barbara took it into her care.

The most famous place of pilgrimage in mediaeval England was Walsingham. Eight crowned heads visited the shrine of Our Lady there, among them Henry VIII, who—before the Reformation—not only visited, but walked the last two miles barefoot. The image of Our Lady of Walsingham was burnt at Chelsea, but in spite of this, Henry on his death-bed commended his soul to her protection. Walsingham was believed to be Our Lady's favourite dwelling place in England, and her shrine shone with precious jewels, metals, and other offerings. Two stone basins near the Chapel of the Virgin, north-east of the conventual church, remain as Erasmus described them. At one time they had a high reputation for the cure of various disorders of the head and stomach. In course of time, like most holy wells, they degenerated into wishing wells, which also have their place in the development of the spas, with their traditional belief in magic, love potions, luck, and other superstitious evasions of personal responsibility. Indeed, we may say that where a holy well becomes a wishing well it has slipped back into the old nature religions.

Walsingham is also of interest in the evolution of ceremonial drinking, which ran through the elaborate methods of water drinking imposed by the doctors we have just discussed to our own toast drinking. The ritual required at Walsingham was very precise. The votary must bare his right knee and place it on a stone between the two basins, throw in a piece of gold and plunge each hand into the water up to the wrists, the left hand into the well on the left, the right hand into the well on the right. The wish must then be clearly formed in the mind, but not uttered, either then or after-wards. This done, the hands must be withdrawn, bringing in their cupped palms as much water as they would hold, and this water be drunk to com-plete the ceremony.

Several of the old wishing wells had the reputation of making those who drank of their water wish either to live in the parish for life, or return to it before death. It is easy to see how a young lady devising how to complete the enslavement of her lover would try to induce him to drink from these. Among such may be mentioned the Ash Well at Kirton Lindsey in Lincoln-shire, the Halliwell at Mavis Enderby, also in Lincolnshire, St. Leonard's Well at Winchelsea in Sussex, and Diana's Well at Wilton in Yorkshire, referred to in the rhyme:

> *Whoever eats Hammer nuts and drinks Diana's watter,*
> *Will never leave Wilton while he's a rag or tatter.*

That the red stain of iron found at chalybeate springs should be mistaken for blood was inevitable, and consequently we find many legends of holy wells originating in death. In Essex we have the legend of St. Osyth's head being struck off by the Danes. Where it fell, the story goes, a fountain gushed forth, which filled the well of the saint, long famous throughout the county for its miraculous cures. The most famous of such wells is in Wales, and therefore outside the scope of this book. But it is so important that it ought at least to be mentioned. It is, of course, the well of St. Winifred in Flintshire. According to the legend, a noble maiden named Winifred was courted by a prince named Cradocus, who, on finding his love spurned, cut off the lady's head. Immediately the earth opened and swallowed up the body of Cradocus; but from the place where the head fell a spring burst from the ground and spread a crimson stain over the stones it covered. St. Bueno, the legend continues, picked up the head and reunited it with the body, after which Winifred lived in sanctity for fifteen years while the water from the spring became renowned for its cures.

The most popular custom still associated with the old holy wells, that of dressing them, has its origin in the Roman festival of Fontanalia, celebrated on the Ides of October in honour of the nymphs of wells and fountains. In his *Ode to the Fountain of Bandusia*, Horace, addressing the fountain, says that it is worthy of offerings of sweet wine and flowers, It is curious that this custom should not have been more widespread. Sir Laurence Gomme, in making his investigations into customs associated with wells, found that in the east of England there was no dressing of wells and little belief in miraculous cures; in Cornwall, offerings and cures; in the North the same; and in the Midlands little belief in cures, but much dressing. Tissington has now the most interesting survival of this romantic custom (67, 68). Ascension Day—or Holy Thursday—each year is kept as a festival, and the five wells of the parish are decorated with elaborately arranged flowers.

Wells and fountains seem to be inalienably linked with the romantic tradition. Often, as we have seen, their very discovery by travellers riding through gloomy forests was in the spirit of the mediaeval romances. Some lines by Sir Walter Scott in *Marmion*, though not strictly applicable, express the mood:

> *Where shall she turn?—behold her mark*
> *A little fountain-cell,*
> *Where water, clear as diamond-spark,*
> *In a stone basin fell.*
> *Above, some half-worn letters say,*
> DRINK · WEARY · PILGRIM · DRINK · AND · PRAY
> FOR · THE · KIND · SOUL · OF · SYBIL · GREY
> WHO · BUILT · THIS · CROSS · AND · WELL.

Fernyhalgh, three miles north of Preston in Lancashire had a holy well with a romantic legend in this tradition associated with it. The story goes that a rich merchant, while crossing the Irish sea, was caught in a storm which tossed the ship he sailed in so angrily that it seemed certain she would break and every man aboard be drowned. Realising the peril they were in, the merchant vowed that if his life was spared he would acknowledge the mercy by doing some pious deed worthy of so great a blessing. As he uttered the vow the storm ceased and the ship came safely to its Lancashire port, whereupon the merchant was admonished by a miraculous voice to seek out a place called Fernyhalgh and discover a well there. Near this well he was ordered to build a chapel. If he did this, said the voice, his vow would be fulfilled. But when the merchant enquired for Fernyhalgh no one could tell him where it was. So he wandered about in search of the place until he came to Preston, and there he put up for the night at an inn a little to the north of the town. The following morning the maid who attended to him was late with breakfast, and in apologising for this she explained that she had been obliged to go in search of a strayed cow, which she had found at Fernyhalgh. Thus the merchant discovered the place of his quest, and when he knelt by the water that morning a figure of the Blessed Virgin appeared before him. The well, therefore, was called Our Lady's Well of Fernyhalgh.

William Harrison, in his *Description of England*, has nothing but scorn for these old stories. Of the holy wells he says, 'Their virtues are now found out to be but baits to draw men and women unto them, either for gaine unto the places where they were, or satisfaction of the lewd disposition of such as hunted after other game.' Seen dispassionately, however, even the stoutest Protestant ought to be able to read in their history something of the slow unveiling of Truth. 'Men are probably nearer to the essential truth in their superstitions than in their science,' said Thoreau. With the growth of modern science the alleged—and indeed well-attested—cures at holy wells were expected to cease. They have not done so. On the contrary, the science that thought to discredit their cures in the seventeenth and eighteenth centuries now appears less credible than the 'superstitions' it scorned. What must now be acknowledged by everyone is that in a mysterious way they have always inspired the most potent factor in any cure—faith.

But with the development of scientific thought in the seventeenth century men became critical of these supernatural waters. That shrewd man Thomas Powell probably spoke for many beside himself when in 1631, in *Tom of All Trades, or the Plain Pathway to Preferment*, he said, 'Let them find out some strange water, some unheard-of spring. It is an easy matter to discolour or alter the taste of it in some measure (it makes no matter how little). Report strange cures that it hath done. Beget a superstitious opinion of it. Good-fellowship shall uphold it, and the neighbouring towns shall all swear for it.' On the other hand, however, we find that moderate and scholarly divine of the day, Bishop Hall, in his *Mystery of Godliness*, writing of a cure performed at St. Madran's Well in Cornwall as 'no less than miraculous.' The suppliant on this occasion had been told in a dream to wash in the well, and Fuller, commenting on Hall's faith in this miracle, says: 'So Authenticall an Author . . . is enough to get belief in any, save, such surly souls, who are resolved on Infidelity of what their own Eyes have not beheld.' Hall and Fuller belong to two generations of transition from the old modes of thought to the new, of which Bacon had been so great a champion. Their belief in old superstitions need not shock or even surprise us. But it does seem strange to learn that even in our own day, according to M. and L.

Quiller-Couch in *The Ancient and Holy Wells of Cornwall*, the West Country Wesleyans are not averse to acknowledging the claims of this particular saint. Of St. Madran's Well the Couches say: 'At the present time people go to the well in crowds on the first Sunday in May, when the Wesleyans hold a service there, and a sermon is preached; after which the people throw in two pins or pebbles to consult the spirit or try for sweethearts. If the two articles sink together, they will soon be married.'

The throwing in of pins is a common custom at wishing wells, especially in Cornwall. Other offerings are in greater favour in the North and Midland counties. Near Newcastle there is a well called Ragwell, because rags were there the offering. At the well of St. Tegla in Denbighshire the votaries were required to walk round the spring three times, repeating the whole of the Lord's Prayer at each circuit, and to lay fourpence on the shrine. A cock or a hen, according to the sex of the suppliant, was then placed in a basket and carried round the well. Afterwards it was taken into the church, where the suppliant had to spend the night under the communion table with a Bible for pillow. If the fowl died before daybreak the disease was believed to have passed into it.

Sir John Floyer (1649-1734), one of the most enlightened of the many who have written on medicinal waters, and historically important as the great advocate of cold water baths, makes it plain that it was the traditional associating of wells with saints that threw them into disuse at the Commonwealth. This he regretted, pointing out that the water itself was put there for man's use and healing by the Creator, who gave the cure, whether indirectly through the saint or directly through the water. Being a doctor in Lichfield, the town of St. Chad, the patron saint of all the wells, Sir John was by no means prejudiced against the older beliefs. It was he, incidentally, who sent Samuel Johnson up to London to be touched for the King's Evil by Queen Anne.

In spite of this overlapping, then, taking the long view there are three distinct phases in the evolution of the spas—that of the pre-Christian pagan wells, that of the holy wells, and that of the spas as we have traced them here. Each has had its rise, its glory, and its decay. Some have passed from one phase into another, adjusting themselves to the new scale of values and being rejuvenated by the fresh life that poured into them. Most of our major spas are now passing into a fourth state. The wheel still turns. Towns, like men, it seems, have their youth, their prime, and their old age. How different was the life in nineteenth-century Cheltenham from that in seventeenth-century Epsom or Tunbridge Wells! At the Restoration the spas, now so respectable in a slightly old-fashioned way, were not unlike our present day holiday-camps, which, however respectable, are certainly not old-fashioned. They were full of gay young people living in tents and enjoying as much freedom as authority would allow, and more if they could take it. Sea-bathing is now substituted for well-bathing, but the spirit is the same, and the waters are for pleasure no less than for healing—if in fact such a distinction can be made.

The life at the early spas was the life of youth—with all the excitement and distress that the love and ambition of youth must always enjoy and suffer by turns. But after a few years the spas also grew up and became sober. Epsom and the earlier Tunbridge Wells gave place to Bath and later to Cheltenham. The carefree became the wilful who prospered and built themselves fine houses, with powdered footmen to wait upon guests who arrived in magnificent coaches and looked noble in their plum-coloured velvet suits and lace cravats; but were no better than the rest underneath. They were puffed up with pride and pretence and for a while they ruled their little world. But in the end nature got the better of them, and after a few years of power they subsided into a peaceful and law-abiding old age, with no greater excitements than the card-table and the trifling gossip of the tea-table could provide. The places that had been frequented, as an old book puts it, by 'ladies that have a desire to be gott with child,' and that in the next age, as Horace Walpole satirically remarked, had put up so many baths that 'One would think that the English were ducks; they are for ever waddling to the waters,' came in the middle of the nineteenth century to be the wealthiest, most feather-bedded places in the kingdom, and at one time were almost entirely deserted by the young, who now went to the seaside resorts for their pleasures. Why, when a theatre was built at Tunbridge Wells in 1901-2 it was called an opera house 'as a concession to parochial propriety'!

But the days of the spas were by no means over. From being watering-places in the literal sense they became places of retirement, particularly with those who had served overseas and in their old age required the kind of climate that Bath and Cheltenham had. Once again the wheel had come full circle. One age had ended and another begun. Britain's overseas expansion had created a new class of people, who, apart from considerations of climate, had lived in the Empire so different a life from that of the workaday England of the normal town and village that on their return they became a separate community. The spas, with their slightly foreign aspect, appealed to them. They appealed also to many in the new leisured class created by the Industrial Revolution at home, particularly to old families who had been driven from their ancestral estates by the spread of factories and were now without roots or local responsibilities. Thus the population of Bath,

Tunbridge Wells, Cheltenham, and Leamington trebled between 1801 and 1851—that is to say, during the period in which the spas were in decline as such, and before the new scientific treatment brought them back into use as centres of healing.

In the spas just named—those of the south and west—life had become elderly and sedate, with the gentlemen spending their mornings in their studies, their afternoons on the sofa, and their evenings at the club. Their children, it is true, still danced; but young men were scarce and inclined to be wary about the numerous widows, who seemed to abound in the spas, and whose chief object in life was to dispose of their daughters successfully.

In the Saloon — (Ladies working — Band playing.)

69 *From a drawing by Randolph Caldecott*

There was as much flirtation as ever; but love required more vigour than could be mustered at the spas in Victorian and Edwardian days. The Bath of Beau Nash, with all its folly, pride, and wit, had ceased to be the resort of aristocracy. It had become, according to a French visitor, 'a sort of great convent... peopled by superannuated celibates of both sexes, but especially women.' Mr. J. A. R. Pimlott, who dealt with the development of both inland and coastal resorts in *The Englishman's Holiday*[1] tells us that in a pamphlet entitled *The Decline and Fall of Bath* the clergy were accused of ruining the city: 'Nothing thrives in Bath nowadays but preaching and praying... the parsons have completely got the whip hand of the good people,' while of Tunbridge Wells, Lady Jerningham in 1806 said: 'The hours are delightful: dinner at four, meeting a little after seven, and parting before eleven, so that Tunbridge is like a large convent, everyone asleep in their beds before twelve.' Yet here the Waters of Scandal had sparkled and turned the heads of those who drank them.

As Epsom and London's country wells were no longer in the running, Tunbridge Wells was again first in the field for the new life created by the Industrial Revolution. Brighton and Hastings had stolen its holiday crowds; but it re-established itself as a prosperous residential town. And this was again done by the enterprise of a business man, who took advantage of the opportunities of his own generation. The new Tunbridge Wells was built by John Ward, through the agency of his architect, Decimus Burton. We may bless or curse them, as we may bless or curse Ralph Allen and the Woods for Bath, or the Duke of Devonshire and John Carr for Buxton, but at least we must recognise that we have persons, and not councils or Government departments, to bless or curse.

The scheme was for nothing less than a new town, with houses, churches, shops, and a market-hall, designed as purposefully to flatter the social aspirations of the nineteenth century as their counterparts had been designed to flatter the social aspirations of the eighteenth. The houses sold quickly; the rest of the scheme was far from successful. Indeed, Victorian Tunbridge Wells was as difficult to launch as Regency Cheltenham had been. Both in their first stages looked more like follies than visions. Time, however, justified them—or at least the greater part of them. The spas had always been designed for a leisurely cultivated life, and leisure was increasing. Town and country had come to terms in them. The short parades at Bath and the Pantiles at Tunbridge Wells, both belonging to an urban rather than a rural tradition, had prepared the way for such breezy walks as those along the Stray at Harrogate and even the Hills at Malvern, while their own more restrained and formal ambitions were splendidly realised in the Promenade at Cheltenham. All moved towards a more expansive lay-out, with parks and wide avenues. Cheltenham, for instance, claims to have thirty thousand lime, chestnut, silver birch, and copper beech trees along twenty-eight miles of avenues, and to have five hundred acres of public parks and open spaces. What wells were to these inland resorts in the eighteenth century, gardens

[1] Faber, 1947.

are to them now—Leamington with its Jephson Gardens, Harrogate with its Valley Gardens, Buxton with its Pavilion Gardens. In these and the fine pavilions that have replaced the old pump-rooms the popular events of their respective seasons are held—Harrogate's Tennis Tournament, Flower and Horse Show, and Northern Counties Athletic Championships meeting; Cheltenham's Festival of British Contemporary Music and Open Competitive Music Festival; Malvern's Drama Festival; as well as all the flower shows, fetes, and gymkhanas that cause such disturbance in Celestial Spheres through so many prayers for fine weather going up in the spas while *Rain, Rain, Rain,* is the farmers' cry.

There are more learned, more virtuous, more industrious towns. There may be happier towns. There are certainly no towns in England more beautiful or more civilised. They were designed and built by men who believed in amenities and proprieties as matters of principle. Those who follow the philosophy of Rousseau, Shelley, Godwin, and their kind, may not have much use for this life regulated by custom and convention—the life of rule. But law and order may be more natural than we suppose. After all, we are more inclined to stick to rules in play than in work, and to get a great deal of fun out of observing them. So it always was in the spas since Beau Nash first made sense out of Folly. George Herbert may hardly seem in character, but the Beau would have agreed with him when he wrote in the *Church Porch*:

> *Slight those who say amidst their sickly healths,*
> *Thou livest by rule. What doth not so but man?*
> *Houses are built by rule, and commonwealths.*
> *Entice the trusty Sun, if that you can,*
> > *From his ecliptic line; beckon the sky.*
> *Who lives by rule then, keeps good company.*

INDEX

The numerals in **heavy type** denote the figure numbers of the illustrations

INDEX

INDEX

George III, King, at Sydenham, 53-4; at Cheltenham, 114-15
Gilsland Spa, 123; **39**
Glastonbury, 123
Gloucester, 123
Goldsmith, Oliver, 10, 46, 64
Gomme, Sir Laurence, 138, 141
Granville, Dr., 117, 126
Greaves, Sir Edward, 132
Grimaldi, Joseph, 34
Guardian, The, 26, 75, 79
Guidott, Dr., 33, 117, 130
Guisborough, 123
Gwyn, Nell, 16, 39

Hail Weston, 121
Hall, Bishop, 142
Hamilton, Count Anthony, 74
Hampstead, 47-50
Hampstead Heath, 47
Hare, Francis, Bishop of Chichester, 6-7
Harrison, William, 4; on Bath, 60, 61; on King's Newman, 121; on holy wells, 142
Harrogate, 4, 94-101; **45, 47, 54;** longevity at, 100
Henrietta Maria, Queen, 22, 121
Hertford, 35
Hill, Sir John, 133-5
Hockley, Essex, 121
Holy Wells, 35-8, 46, 94, 108, 121, 123-4, 137-43
Holywell, Shoreditch, 36
Horley Green, 123
Huntingdon, Selina, Countess of, 70

Ilkley, 123
Ipswich, 122
Irving, Washington, 46
Islington Spa, 30-2; **18**

James I, King, 46, 130
Jenner, Dr., 114
Jennings, Charles, quoted, 30
Johnson, Samuel, on the queen and Mrs. Thrale, 43; at Welwyn, 47; at Streatham, **55;** at Bath, 71;

on Dr. Hill, 134; on Dr. Cheyne, 135; touched for the King's Evil, 143
Jones, Dr. John, 4, 86
Jonson, Ben, 41, 76
Jorden, Dr. Edward, 130
Josselin, Ralph, 87

Keats, John, 50
Ken, Bishop, 87
Kensington, 42
Keyse, Thomas, 42
Kilburn Wells, 46
King, Tom, 34
King's Cross, 35, 38, 46
King's Newman, near Coventry, 121
Kirton Lindsey, Lincs, 140
Kit Cat Club, at Hampstead, 49-50
Knaresborough, 94, 96; **46**

Lamb, Charles, 47
Lambe, Dr., 118
Lambeth, 42-3
Lansdown, Bath, 123, 124
Leamington, 116-19; **53**
Le Blanc, Abbé, 3, 83
Leeds, 123
Leicester, Earl of, 88
Leland, John, itinerary of, 60, 124
Lennard, Reginald, 27
Levingstone, Dr., 17, 20
Lichfield, 143
Little, Bryan, 69, 112
London and Bath Royal Patent Steam Coach, **24**
London, country wells, 44-57; spas, 30-43
London Spaw, 30, 41
London Spy, The, 77
Ludgate Hill, 35
Lydgate's *Falls of Princes,* 2
Lyson's *Environs of London,* 50

Macaulay, Lord, 20, 70
Macky, John, 5, 20
Madan, Dr., 2, 5
Malton, 123
Malvern, 37, 106-10; **51, 52**
Malvern Festival, 110

INDEX